AROUND THE WORLD
IN
CROSS STITCH

AROUND THE WORLD
IN
CROSS STITCH

JAN EATON

Trafalgar
Square

First published in the United States of America in 1994 by
Trafalgar Square Publishing, North Pomfret, Vermont 05053

ISBN 0-943955-85-8
Library of Congress Catalog Card Number: 93-60907

Editor: ELIZABETH ROWE
Designer: PETER BRIDGEWATER
Cover designer: PETER BRIDGEWATER
Photographer: STEVE TANNER
Illustrators: SIMONE END, GEOFF DENNEY, DEBRA WOODWARD
Phototypeset by CENTRAL SOUTHERN TYPESETTERS, EASTBOURNE
Originated by P&W GRAPHICS PTE LTD
Printed and bound in Singapore by TIEN WAH PTE LTD

ACKNOWLEDGEMENTS

The author would like to thank the following:

- DMC for supplying embroidery fabrics and threads
- Framecraft for supplying needlework accessories
- MacGregor Designs for supplying the footstool on page 134
- Cara Ackerman of DMC Creative World
- Wendy Bailey
- John Goodall for his imaginative picture framing
- Mike Gray of Framecraft

and the following friends and colleagues for lending props from around the
world for photography:

- Penny Adams • Nigel Benson • Bill Burnett • Annette Claxton
- Sue Duffy • Jo Finnis • Pat Hornsey • Charlotte Parry-Crooke
- Ingrid Renshawe-Strack • Lizzy Rowe • Clare Royals • Amy Speak

The wooden tray and crystal vase (page 25), crystal bowl and jar (pages 40–41),
wooden bowls (page 104), porcelain boxes (page 129) and dressing table set
(pages 142–3) are available by mail order from the following Framecraft suppliers:
Anne Brinkley Design, 761 Palma Avenue, Holmdel, NJ 07733,
Phone: (908) 787-2011; Gay Bowles Sales, Inc., PO Box 1060, Janesville,
WI 53547, Phone: (800) 356-9438.

DMC embroidery fabrics and threads are widely available. For further
information contact The DMC Corporation, 10 Port Kearny, South Kearny,
NJ 07032, Phone: (201) 589-0606.

CONTENTS

INTRODUCTION

INTRODUCTION

Around the World in Cross Stitch contains over fifty original projects for cross stitch embroidery featuring designs from right round the globe, many of which have been inspired by the traditional arts and crafts of a particular country or region. The wide range of design sources illustrates the almost limitless possibilities of this form of counted thread embroidery. Cross stitch is a very old technique of fabric decoration and examples of the craft exist in almost every country across the world, worked by both peasant women and professional embroiderers. This diversity is well represented in the choice of projects, which cover a range of practical and decorative items from an apron with an African theme to a simple, gathered skirt decorated with a braid- and lace-trimmed Eastern European peasant border and a set of useful porcelain boxes featuring miniature designs inspired by the painted architecture of ancient Egypt.

The projects have been divided into nine chapters, each one containing designs influenced by a particular geographical region. Each chapter is introduced and illustrated with text and pictures which will give you a flavour of the region and provide interesting background information about the inspiration behind the project designs. This introductory section not only covers the relevant history, development and natural features of the region, but it also describes local traditions of decorative arts and crafts. Included in each introduction are practical hints for alternative ways of using the project charts and selecting the different methods of embroidering cross stitch.

A section at the end of each introduction suggests many more sources of ethnic designs from the region and encourages you to investigate further, guiding you through historical design styles, buildings, costume, pottery and other artifacts to more general subjects which you can read more about in your local library or museum. Ethnological and travel books will provide further information, as will magazines and the glossy, picture-filled brochures advertising holidays in exotic, far-away places. The scope of ethnic designs is so vast that you will quickly begin to make a useful collection of visual references and perhaps feel inspired to begin to create your own charts for cross stitch with the help of graphed tracing paper or a set of grid-printed acetate sheets. You may decide to specialize in just one region,

perhaps choosing Western Europe or the Far East, or to concentrate instead on the ancient civilizations of Egypt, Greece and Rome or the New World empires of the Maya, Inca and Aztec.

Keep all the information you gather filed neatly away for future use. Label magazine cuttings with any relevant information as soon as you cut them out and keep the cuttings in stiff cardboard files to prevent them becoming creased and dog-eared. A collection of postcards can provide a great deal of visual information in miniature form, especially if you and your family and friends like to travel and send cards back home. Post-

on page 24, the Aboriginal creatures picture (page 94) and the Persian tiles notebook (page 124) are for expert stitchers. These projects require a great deal of concentration and dedication to stitch successfully, but the finished results will give you lasting pleasure.

The projects are interspersed with pattern library pages which contain a wealth of charted designs centred around one particular theme. For example, the pattern library on page 119 which follows the Chinese bedlinen project provides you with a stylish Chinese-style alphabet so that you can add initials or a monogram to your embroidered bedlinen. Some of the pattern library pages contain a mixture of motifs, borders and all-over patterns in different sizes. These can be stitched directly on to evenweave fabric using the colour combinations shown, or the charts can be adapted to suit your own purposes. You will find helpful hints on adapting existing charts on page 162. Many of the project charts can also be used in different ways. The delicate orchid and trellis pattern from the dressing table set on page 142 would look charming across a cushion cover if it was stitched in slightly stronger colors on a pale pink or green fabric, while the stylized Tunisian camels (page 126) are highly suitable for use as a border across the bottom of a fluffy cream, apricot or beige bath towel. Don't be afraid to experiment with color, changing fabric and thread colors as you please, but always try out a small sample of your new colorway to check the effect before you start a large project.

To make one of the projects illustrated in the book, look through the pages and make your selection, bearing in mind your own level of skill. Read through the list of materials and the written instructions carefully and be sure you understand each step before proceeding to the next. Technical terms are explained in the glossary on page 174 and the practical processes involved are fully discussed and illustrated in Chapter 10 at the back of the book. This chapter contains useful basic information about the types of fabric and threads which are available and how to work a piece of cross stitch embroidery square-by-square from a charted design. It also explains in detail the process of scaling up and cutting out paper patterns and how to construct the garments featured in some of the projects.

THIS COLLECTION of cross stitch embroideries and pieces of decorated china incorporates design motifs from around the world.

cards are easily stored in shoe boxes or large card-index files complete with subject dividers.

The projects illustrated in *Around the World in Cross Stitch* will suit everybody from beginners to experts. The small, easy-to-work projects like the Polynesian bowls on page 103 and the Asante bookmark (page 85) are ideal for the beginner, while the more complicated designs such as the Christmas heirloom on page 27 and the Gujarati shoulder bag (page 140) would be perfect for a stitcher with previous experience of working cross stitch from a charted design or commercial kit. The largest, most complex projects including the Assisi tray

CHAPTER ONE

WESTERN EUROPE

The many civilizations and cultures of ancient and modern Western Europe are full of sources of designs for all kinds of embroidery including cross stitch, from geometric to floral and abstract to symbolic. The designs in this chapter reflect this diversity, and they range in scope from Elizabethan England to medieval Italy and present-day Germany.

The Elizabethan herb bags on page 14 are ideal projects for someone who is relatively new to the craft of embroidery. Each of the three designs is worked on a separate piece of evenweave fabric, then the finished embroideries are bonded on to printed cotton using fusible webbing and a hot iron. The embroidered panels are finished off with a border of blanket stitch worked in pink thread to match the embroidery before the bag is made up. The three designs are inspired by Elizabethan band samplers, which are some of the earliest forms of sampler stitching in existence. Band samplers were usually long and narrow in shape and were worked by the needlewoman as a way of practising new designs and stitches which were arranged in horizontal bands across the sampler. A further selection of designs from Elizabethan samplers is given in the pattern library on page 17, and these can be used to make your own band sampler. Follow the guidelines given on page 162 to help you plan and stitch your sampler.

Tartan, a fabric woven with a distinctive check-like pattern which is created by straight lines of color crossing at right angles, formed part of the everyday dress of the people of Scotland for many centuries. Gradually, its use developed until the fabric became a symbol of clan kinship, particularly amongst the close-knit families living in the Highlands, and tartan fabric was fashioned into kilts, belted plaids and trews. After the Jacobites were defeated at the Battle of Culloden in 1746, the British government passed an Act of Parliament disarming the Highland Scots and forbidding the wearing of tartan. By the time this act was repealed in 1785, tartan was almost a thing of the past: many of the tartan weavers had died and most of the original patterns were lost. However, by 1822, the custom of wearing tartan began to revive and many new patterns were invented to replace those which had disappeared. Today, tartans are firmly back in favour and are worn all over the world.

The waistcoat on page 18 is decorated with a tartan pattern based on the traditional green, blue and red plaid worn by the Duncan clan, and a further selection

of all-over tartan designs is given on page 20. Tartan designs look very effective when worked on evenweave fabric, particularly when a strongly colored fabric is used as the background and portions of this are left unstitched to become integral parts of the design. The waistcoat in the photograph is designed in a short, boxy style and the pattern provided on page 155 will fit a size 10. You may prefer to buy a commercial waistcoat pattern in a different shape or size. In this case, be sure to choose a simple shape without darts or complicated shaping, and be sure to work the pattern outwards from the centre of the front piece.

The elaborate interlaced patterns found on ancient Celtic wood and stone carvings, illuminated manuscripts and jewellery are often known as 'the work of angels' because of their complexity. The distinctive knots, spirals and plaits of this art form have been a source of inspiration for artists, illustrators and textile designers throughout the centuries. Two alternative designs, an all-over pattern and a simple border, are provided with the project and either can be used to decorate the christening gown on page 21, or you may like to substitute one of the designs shown in the pattern library on page 23.

Assisi embroidery is named after the town of Assisi in Italy which was the home of St Francis, the founder of the Franciscan order of monks, who was well known for his love of birds and animals. In 1980, St Francis was proclaimed the patron saint of ecology. Assisi embroidery is typified by the use of two thread colours to work designs in cross stitch and Holbein stitch. The designs usually feature natural subjects like plants, birds and animals. The background areas are first filled in with cross stitch and then outlined with a dark color, leaving the design elements unworked. Traditionally,

the cross stitch areas were embroidered in shades of blue, terracotta or red on a white or natural linen background, then the shapes were outlined in dark grey or black. The tray on page 24 features a design of plants and flowers stitched in traditional terracotta and dark grey, but this design would look equally effective worked in bright thread colors on a dark fabric. A selection of Assisi motifs and borders is given in the pattern library on page 26.

In many countries of Western Europe, the coming of Christmas is heralded every year by the giving of family Advent calendars to young children at the beginning of December. The Christmas heirloom on page 27, complete with a tiny, gift-wrapped parcel for each day, is based on a German calendar and it can be used year after year by simply adding new gifts below each number. You could decorate the calendar by adding several of the Christmas motifs shown on page 29, or personalize the gift by embroidering the child's name using the alphabet on the same page.

You may like to explore the rich heritage of Western Europe further, perhaps with a view to creating and charting your very own, totally unique designs for cross stitch. There are hints to help you make your own charts on page 162, and information on different types of fabric and threads on page 158. You could begin by exploring some of the following sources: the colorful and intricate mosaics of ancient Rome and Byzantium; medieval stained glass in Europe's great cathedrals; timeless blue and white Delft chinaware; formal patterns of Italian gardens and French châteaux parterres; Elizabethan knot and herb gardens; plants and flowers from English country cottage gardens; paintings, illustrations, jewellery and other designed objects produced during the Art Nouveau period; Gaudi's architecture in Barcelona; William Morris and the Arts and Crafts Movement.

WESTERN EUROPEAN cultures encompass the ceremonial customs of ancient monarchies and contemporary republics, laced with a rich vein of lively folk tradition.

ELIZABETHAN
HERB BAGS

Since the earliest times, bags of sweet-smelling, dried herbs, petals and flower heads have been used to protect stored bedding and other household linens against the ravages of moths and to add fragrance. Fill these decorated bags with lavender, rose petals or chamomile, according to your taste.

MATERIALS

- Small pieces of antique white 18 count Ainring evenweave fabric 51 in (130 cm) wide (Zweigart E3793, color 101)
- Printed fine cotton fabric with a design in pinks and greens
- Pink satin ribbon ¼ in (6 mm) wide
- DMC stranded cotton in the following colors: pinks 3350, 3608, 3716, 3733; purple 327; red 915; turquoise 564; greens 702, 907, 991
- Tapestry needle size 24
- Crewel needle size 8
- Fusible bonding web
- Tacking thread in a dark color
- Sewing needle and pins
- Sewing thread to match the background color of the printed fabric
- Embroidery hoop
- Knitting needle
- Pinking scissors
- Dried lavender/rose petals/chamomile

PREPARING THE FABRIC

You will need one piece of evenweave fabric and two pieces of printed cotton for each herb bag you make. First, tack vertical and horizontal lines on the evenweave fabric to correspond with the size of each motif, taking care to leave sufficient extra fabric all round to allow you to mount the fabric in the hoop. Next, fold each piece in four and mark the centres with a pin or a few tacking stitches. Mark the centre of each chart with a soft pencil.

CHOOSE STRONGLY SCENTED fillings such as dried lavender, rose petals or chamomile to scent your household linens.

Alternatively, fill the bags with dried hops and keep one under your pillow to ensure a restful night's sleep.

WORKING THE EMBROIDERY

1 Mount the fabric in the embroidery hoop (page 160). Begin working the flower motifs in cross stitch (page 164) from the chart, using three strands of thread in the needle throughout and noting that each square on the chart represents one cross stitch worked over two vertical and two horizontal woven blocks of fabric.

2 Next, work the linear details in back stitch (page 164), again using three strands of thread and working each stitch over two fabric blocks.

MAKING UP THE HERB BAGS

1 Press the embroidery lightly on the wrong side over a well-padded surface. Use a warm iron and take care not to crush the stitching.

2 Following the manufacturer's instructions carefully, iron a piece of fusible bonding web on to the back of each embroidery. When the pieces are cool, cut away the surplus fabric, leaving a margin of six blocks of fabric round the design.

3 Peel away the backing paper from the motifs and, following the diagram on page 152, position each one on the right side of a piece of printed cotton. Press the motifs with a steam iron (or an ordinary iron and a damp cloth) to secure them.

4 Work a row of blanket stitch (page 166) round each motif, using two strands of the appropriate pink thread in the crewel needle. Work the upright stitch over two fabric blocks and space the stitches evenly round the edge of the fabric, keeping them two blocks apart.

5 Place the front and back pieces of the printed cotton together with right sides facing and machine stitch round three sides, leaving the top open. Clip the corners (page 169) and turn the bag right side out, taking care to push each corner out gently with the point of the knitting needle.

6 Fill each bag approximately two-thirds full with the appropriate filling, cut across the top using pinking scissors, then secure the bag with a length of pink satin ribbon tied in a bow.

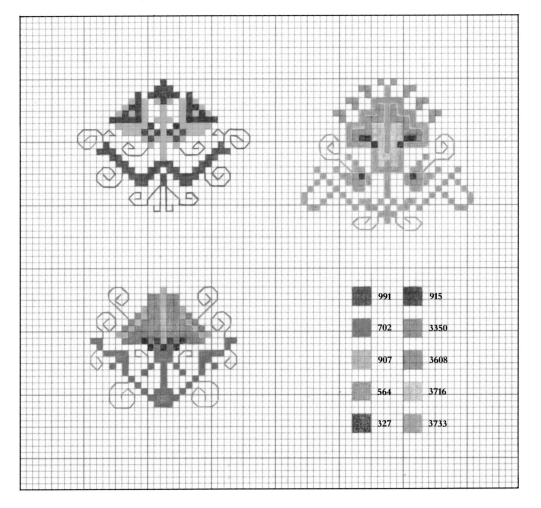

991	915
702	3350
907	3608
564	3716
327	3733

EACH COLORED square on the chart represents one cross stitch worked over two vertical and two horizontal woven blocks of fabric. The linear details are worked in back stitch, also over two fabric blocks.

ELIZABETHAN PATTERN LIBRARY

TARTAN
WAISTCOAT

The tartan pattern on this stylish cropped waistcoat is quick to embroider in half cross stitch, with the un-stitched areas of green fabric forming an integral part of the design. A selection of alternative tartan patterns is shown in chart form on page 20.

MATERIALS

- Dark green 18 count Ainring evenweave fabric 51 in (130 cm) wide (Zweigart E3793, color 685 Christmas green)
- Red silk or polyester lining fabric
- DMC stranded cotton in the following colors: red 600; kingfisher 996; blue 798; white
- Tapestry needle size 24
- Tacking thread in a light color
- Dark green sewing thread
- Sewing needle and pins
- Adjustable rectangular embroidery frame and embroidery hoop
- Dressmaker's pattern paper

PREPARING THE FABRIC

Make a paper pattern of the waistcoat by enlarging the diagrams on page 155 to the required size and cutting the back, front and pocket pieces out of dressmaker's paper. Lay the left front piece on the right side of the evenweave fabric and mark the area to be embroidered by tacking round the outside close to the edge of the paper. Repeat with the pocket. You will need to leave a margin of at least 4 in (10 cm) all round each piece to allow the fabric to be mounted in the frame or hoop. Cut the back and the right front pieces out of evenweave fabric and mark the position of the pocket with tacking. Cut out the lining.

WORKING THE EMBROIDERY

LEFT FRONT

1 Tack a vertical line through the centre of the tacked shape, taking care not to cross any vertical threads. Mark the central horizontal line in the same way. You have now marked the centre of your embroidery. Mount the fabric in the embroidery frame (page 161).

2 Beginning at the centre marked on the fabric, work the repeating tartan pattern in half cross stitch (page 165) from the chart, using three strands of thread in the

needle throughout. Work outwards from the X on the chart, remembering that each square on the chart represents a half cross stitch worked over two vertical and two horizontal woven blocks of fabric. Continue stitching until the area inside the tacked lines is covered with the tartan pattern.

POCKET

Working in the same way as for the left front, mount the fabric in the hoop and work the band of pattern

indicated on the chart in half cross stitch across the top of the pocket.

MAKING UP THE WAISTCOAT

1 Press the embroidery lightly on the wrong side over a well-padded surface. Use a warm iron and take care not to crush the stitching.

2 Cut out the embroidered pieces along the tacked lines and follow the illustrated steps shown on page 152 for making and lining the waistcoat.

THE PATTERN shown on page 155 will make a size 10 cropped waistcoat. If you would like to make a different size or style of waistcoat, buy a commercial paper pattern and work the embroidery in the same way, but avoid using a complicated pattern containing darts or fancy shaping.

TARTAN PATTERN LIBRARY

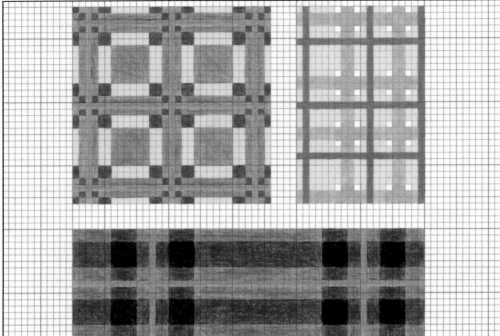

EACH COLORED square represents a half cross stitch worked over two vertical and two horizontal woven blocks of fabric. The colored lines indicate the pattern repeat and also show the section of the design which fits across the pocket top.

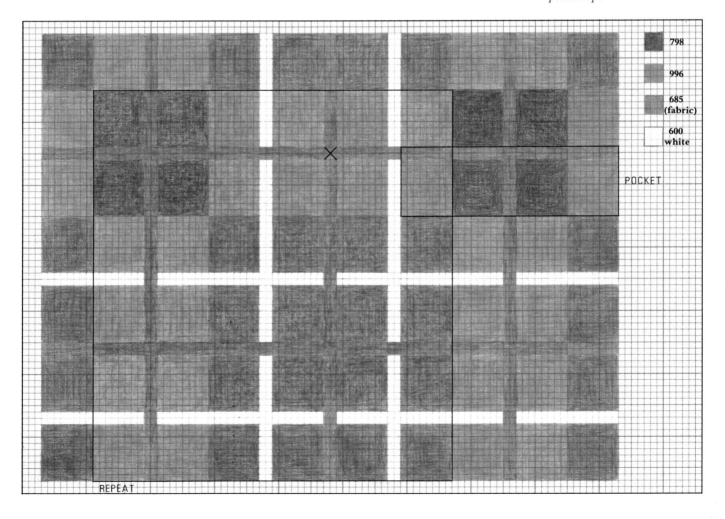

	798
	996
	685 (fabric)
	600 white

POCKET

X

REPEAT

CELTIC
CHRISTENING GOWN

Inspired by the twisting and twining knots and plaits of centuries-old Celtic stone carving and metalwork, a simple interlaced pattern is embroidered in pastel shades to decorate the yoke of this pretty christening gown.

MATERIALS

- Small piece of white 11 count Damask Aida even-weave fabric 67 in (170 cm) wide (Zweigart E3238, color 1)
- Fine white cotton fabric with a self-pattern
- White satin bias binding and narrow elastic
- DMC stranded cotton in the following colors: pink 3716; yellow 743; blue 794; green 564
- Tapestry needle size 24
- Tacking thread in a dark color
- Matching sewing thread
- Sewing needle and pins
- Embroidery hoop
- Dressmaker's pattern paper

PREPARING THE FABRIC

Make a paper pattern of the christening gown by enlarging the diagrams on page 154 to the required size and cutting the pieces out of dressmaker's paper. Lay the yoke piece on the right side of the evenweave fabric and mark the area to be embroidered by tacking round the outside of the shape close to the edge of the paper. You will need to leave a margin of at least 4 in (10 cm) all round the yoke to allow the fabric to be mounted in the hoop. Cut the remaining pattern pieces out of the cotton fabric, following the cutting layout.

WORKING THE EMBROIDERY

1 Tack a vertical line through the centre of the tacked shape, taking care not to cross any vertical threads. Mark the central horizontal line in the same way and mark the centre of the chart with a soft pencil. Mount the fabric in the embroidery hoop (page 160).

2 Beginning at the centre of the tacked shape, work the repeating interlaced pattern in cross stitch (page 164) from the chart, using three strands of thread in the needle throughout. Work outwards until the area inside the tacked lines is covered with stitching. Remember that each square on the chart represents one cross stitch worked over one woven block of fabric.

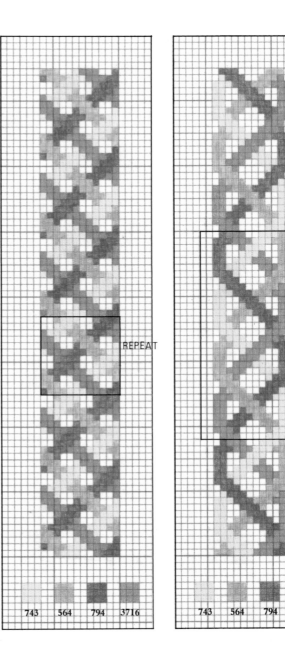

| 743 | 564 | 794 | 3716 |

| 743 | 564 | 794 | 3716 |

A VARIATION of the design is shown on the second chart. Here, the interlacing pattern forms a border, which can be used in a band across the yoke instead of the original all-over pattern. The more experienced stitcher can use the waste canvas technique shown on page 163 to work either of the yoke designs.

MAKING UP THE CHRISTENING GOWN

1 Remove the embroidery from the hoop and press lightly on the wrong side over a well-padded surface. Use a warm iron and take care not to crush the stitching.

2 Cut out the embroidered yoke along the tacked outline and follow the illustrated steps shown on page 153 for making up the gown.

THE PATTERN *shown on page 154 will make a christening gown to fit a baby up to three months old. If you would like to make a larger size, buy a commercial paper pattern for a* similar christening gown, then work the embroidery across the yoke as shown here. When selecting fabric, choose one made from pure cotton in white or ivory.

CELTIC PATTERN LIBRARY

ASSISI
TRAY

A wooden tray, specially designed to show off fine needlework, makes the perfect setting for an Assisi design worked in terracotta and grey. This type of embroidery, in which the background is filled in with cross stitch while the design elements are left unworked, comes originally from the town of Assisi in central Italy.

MATERIALS

- Antique white 18 count Ainring evenweave fabric 51 in (130 cm) wide (Zweigart E3793, color 101)
- Sudberry House petite tray WPS (available from Framecraft, see page 4)
- DMC stranded cotton in the following colors: terracotta 351; dark grey 3799
- Tapestry needle size 24
- Tacking thread in a dark color
- Sewing needle
- Large embroidery hoop or adjustable rectangular embroidery frame
- Dressmaker's pattern paper

MEASURING UP

Carefully unscrew one end of the tray and slide out the glass, card mat, backing board and wooden insert with oval aperture. The oval aperture measures 10¼ in × 7 in (26 cm × 18 cm), so you will need a piece of evenweave fabric slightly larger all round than this. Don't forget to add at least 4 in (10 cm) extra all round to allow you to mount the fabric in your hoop or frame.

PREPARING THE FABRIC

To make a paper pattern, lay the wooden insert over a piece of dressmaker's pattern paper and draw round the oval aperture with a pencil. Cut out the pattern and place it on the right side of the evenweave fabric. Mark the oval shape on the fabric with a line of tacking. Then tack a vertical line through the centre of the tacked outline, taking care not to cross any vertical threads. Mark the central horizontal line in the same way and mark the centre of the chart with a soft pencil. Mount the fabric in the embroidery hoop or frame (page 160).

WORKING THE EMBROIDERY

1 Begin working the design in cross stitch (page 164) from the centre of the fabric. Use three strands of thread

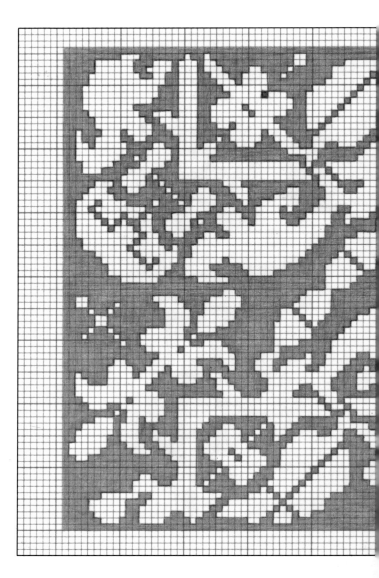

and note that each colored square represents one cross stitch worked over two vertical and two horizontal woven blocks of fabric. Continue the embroidery over the tacked outline by about ½ in (1.5 cm) to avoid gaps in the stitching when the tray is reassembled.

2 Outline each portion of the design with a row of Holbein stitch (page 164) in two strands of grey.

MAKING UP THE TRAY

1 When all the embroidery has been completed, press the fabric lightly on the wrong side over a well-padded surface. Use a warm iron and take care not to press too hard and crush the stitching.

2 Cut out the fabric to the required size, allowing a margin of 1 in (2.5 cm) outside the tacked lines all round the oval. Centre the embroidery on the card mat and secure it with sticky tape.

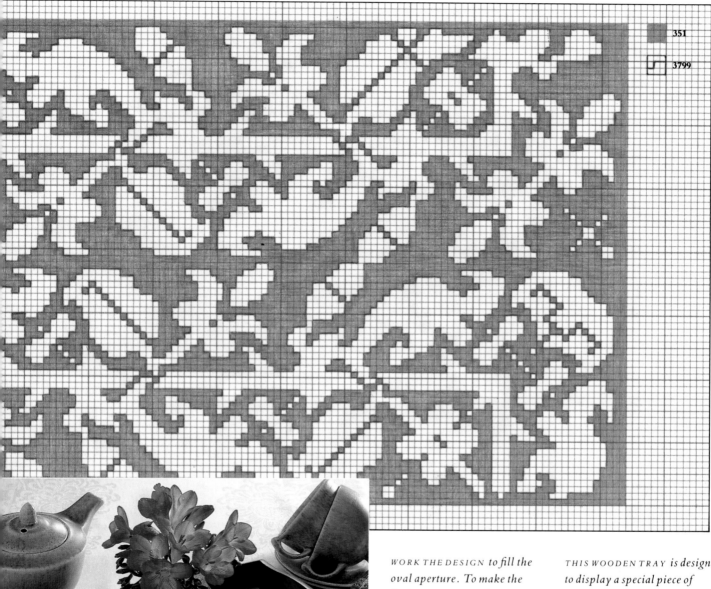

351

3799

WORK THE DESIGN *to fill the oval aperture. To make the design more versatile, the chart has been continued beyond the oval shape required by the tray to create a rectangular design.*

THIS WOODEN TRAY *is designed to display a special piece of embroidery. The stitching is protected from everyday dirt and spills by a sheet of glass underneath a wooden insert.*

3 Clean both sides of the glass. Lay the backing board on a flat surface, then cover it with the card mat (right side of the embroidery uppermost), the glass and the wooden insert.

4 Separate the frame slightly, slide the assembled layers into the side grooves and gently push them into place. Reassemble the end of the tray.

ASSISI PATTERN LIBRARY

CHRISTMAS
HEIRLOOM

Make this German Advent calendar to celebrate the coming of Christmas. There is a tiny, gift-wrapped parcel or chocolate decoration to unwrap every day during December until Christmas Day finally arrives. To use the calendar in future years, bring it out of storage and add new gifts.

MATERIALS

- Pale green 11 count Pearl Aida evenweave fabric 43 in (110 cm) wide (Zweigart E1007, color 617 mint)
- DMC stranded cotton in the following colors: pink 335; purple 208; red 666; orange 947; yellow 444; kingfisher 996; blues 796, 3760; green 702; tan 976
- Narrow green and red satin ribbon
- Empty matchboxes or other small boxes
- Small gifts
- Wrapped chocolate Christmas decorations
- 24 small brass curtain or tie-back rings
- Metallic Christmas wrapping paper
- Tapestry needle size 24
- Tacking thread in a dark color
- Bright red sewing thread
- Sewing needle and pins
- Adjustable rectangular embroidery frame or large embroidery hoop
- Sturdy cardboard
- Strong linen carpet thread or very fine string

MEASURING UP

The embroidered area of the Advent calendar measures approximately 15 in × 21¾ in (38 cm × 55 cm), but you will need to add at least 8 in (20 cm) all round to allow for mounting the fabric in a frame to work the stitching and so that the finished embroidery can be laced round card prior to framing.

PREPARING THE FABRIC

Cut out the fabric to the required size. Using the photograph as a guide, scatter the gifts randomly across the fabric, marking the position of each one with a pin. When you are happy with the arrangement, mark the position of each number above a gift with rows of tacking, making sure you include every number from 1 to 24. Remove the gifts and the pins. Mount the fabric in the embroidery frame or hoop.

THE NUMBERS are arranged at random on the calendar, then stitched in the appropriate colors from the chart. Each colored square represents one cross stitch worked over one fabric block. Outline all the numbers with a row of back stitch, except those colored dark blue.

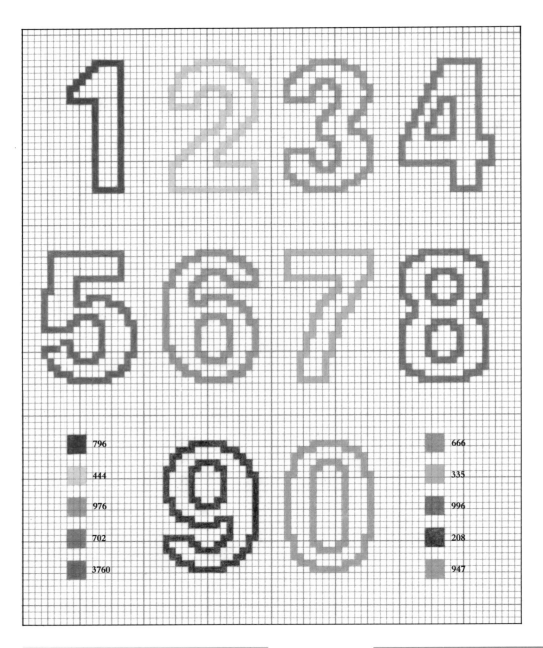

■ 796	■ 666
■ 444	■ 335
■ 976	■ 996
■ 702	■ 208
■ 3760	■ 947

FILL EACH PARCEL with a tiny gift to delight a child. For a girl, choose a length of pretty hair ribbon, tiny dolls, a bead necklace and bracelet or toy cosmetics. For a boy, collect small cars and trucks, dice and counters, marbles or fun erasers. When your inspiration runs out, fill any empty parcels with sweets, brightly colored balloons or a folded tissue paper party hat.

WORKING THE EMBROIDERY

1 Stitch each number individually in cross stitch (page 164), noting that each colored square on the chart represents one complete stitch worked over one woven block of fabric. Use three strands of thread in the needle throughout.

2 Work carefully from the chart, stopping at intervals to check that the individual components are spaced correctly and that the top diagonal of each stitch faces in the same direction.

3 Outline each number (except those stitched in dark blue) with a row of back stitch (page 164) using two strands of dark blue 796 in the needle.

FINISHING THE ADVENT CALENDAR

1 Press the embroidery lightly on the wrong side over a well-padded surface. Use a warm iron and take care not to press down too hard and crush the stitching.

2 Using red sewing thread, attach a ring below each number. Lace the embroidery (page 173) securely over a piece of sturdy card cut to the appropriate size. Use strong linen carpet thread or very fine string for the lacing. Follow the suggestions given on page 173 for having your embroidery framed.

3 Place the gifts in the boxes, wrap them with paper and tie them with ribbon. Finally, attach a wrapped gift or chocolate decoration to each ring.

CHRISTMAS PATTERN LIBRARY

CHAPTER TWO

EASTERN EUROPE

The arts and crafts of Eastern Europe are characterized by bold, colorful shapes and designs with a 'peasant' feel, many of which have been handed down through the generations from mother to daughter. Embroidery has always been a flourishing craft in this area, and its use is widespread in decorating household linens such as tablecloths and the ends of towels as well as in traditional costumes for both men and women. Cross stitch, together with its many variations such as long-armed cross stitch and other counted thread stitches, features strongly in the indigenous textile crafts, probably due to the predominance of flax cultivation in this area of the world. The flax fibres are spun to make linen thread and this is woven, often by hand, into fabric which is used as an embroidery background. The fabric is often left in its natural, unbleached state or it can be bleached to produce a snowy white fabric with a lustrous sheen.

Throughout the Balkans, an area consisting of present-day Greece, Albania, what was Yugoslavia, Bulgaria and certain parts of Romania and Turkey, much of the antique and modern cross stitch embroidery is heavily stylized and based on repeating flower, fruit and leaf motifs. In Bulgaria, for instance, cross stitch flower motifs are often outlined with black, rather in the manner of Assisi embroidery, with small 'hook' shapes breaking out of the outlines at right angles.

The Balkan place setting on page 34 is based on this type of design, but here it is worked in bright colors of thread rather than in the traditional color combination of red thread on white or natural linen fabric. The matching tablemat and napkin are suitable for a relative beginner to attempt, and the set will provide valuable practice in following a simple border chart made up of repeating elements. The more experienced needlewoman could stitch the repeating border round the edge of a square or rectangular tablecloth, turning the corners neatly with the help of a small mirror, as shown on page 162. Two similar border designs, also based on Balkan embroideries, can be found at the top of the pattern library on page 38. All three borders can be used together, positioned one above the other, to make a deep band across a cushion cover or to decorate the hem of a simple, gathered skirt.

Traditional Eastern European folk costumes for both men and women are colorfully decorated with complex embroidered patterns, applied ribbons and woven braids, spangles, lace and frills. Although the wearing of this type of costume has declined during the latter part of this century, women in many parts of Eastern Europe still display their traditional skills by embroidering blouses and other garments for sale in Western Europe and the United States of America. The embroidered designs on these garments, although often lacking the spontaneity and liveliness of the true peasant costumes, show a high degree of expertise with their cross stitch motifs and intricately repeating borders.

The border design on page 36 reflects this colorful peasant embroidery in the way it combines cross stitch, woven flower-patterned braids and crisp white lace set

off against a deep green background. Mixing three common design elements from Eastern Europe, birds, hearts and flowers, the cross stitch border is straight-forward to stitch, providing you take care to space the elements out correctly. Work the embroidery first, then add rows and rows of colorful woven braids above and below the border. Here, the braids have been machine stitched in position with matching thread, but you can apply them by hand if you prefer, either by slipstitching (page 168) them to the background or by securing them with rows of blanket stitch (page 166) worked in a contrasting color. Four more peasant border designs are given in the pattern library on page 38, and any of these can be used with braid and lace in the same way or the borders can be combined in multiple rows to make a deeper band

of embroidery.

In the Kalocsa region of Hungary, wooden furniture and interior walls are often decorated with floral bouquets, swags and wreaths. The furniture is usually carved, then painted with patterns of stylized roses and tulips using oil colors. The wall decorations are painted by the women of the town or village, using powdered pigments mixed to a paste to create colorful designs on interior walls first covered with smooth, whitewashed plaster. Although each painter has her own distinct style, several women will work together decorating the same wall. The decorations, like those on the furniture, are also floral, but here many more different species are combined: roses, tulips, pansies, lilies and forget-me-nots, foxgloves and poppies, cornflowers and acacia blossoms rub shoulders with golden ears of ripe corn and green leaves.

The exuberant rose designs decorating the crystal jars on page 40 sprang from this source. Here, two sizes of rose and leaf motifs are embroidered on sparkling white fabric, then set in silver-plated lids which top hand-cut lead crystal containers. The surface of the embroidery is protected from dirt by a covering of transparent acetate. More rose designs are given in the pattern library on page 39: two large roses which can be used singly to decorate a cushion cover or stitched as a pair of pictures are flanked by both small and large motifs and several border designs.

The brightly colored love token on page 42 reflects the Eastern European fascination with heart and flower designs. The central portion of the design was inspired by a particularly fine piece of floral satin stitch embroidery and this has been enclosed in a simple heart outline stitched in red. Here, the embroidery has been mounted inside a double wooden frame painted to match two of the thread colors, but you could also show off your stitching by turning the design into a greetings card to mark a special occasion.

You may like to explore the following suggestions and design your own Eastern European patterns: Russia's cossack heritage and costume embroideries; silver jewellery from Montenegro; the floral painted tinware of Eastern European gypsies; peasant figure motifs from Poland; designs for the Ballets Russes by Bakst and Diaghilev; Russian icons; Khokhloma folk painting; Czechoslovakian cutwork embroidery.

FROM THE onion domes of Moscow to the traditional peasant embroideries, Eastern European arts are characterized by bold shapes and strong colors.

BALKAN
PLACE SETTING

A charming flower and leaf border and motif decorate this matching tablemat and napkin. Inspired by the red and white embroideries found in the Balkan countries, this colorful and intricate design uses a combination of cross stitch and back stitch.

MATERIALS

- Pale blue 16 count Aida evenweave fabric 43 in (110 cm) wide (Zweigart E3251, color 550 sky)
- DMC stranded cotton in the following colors: red 600; yellow 307; blue 796; green 701
- Tapestry needle size 24
- Matching sewing thread
- Tacking thread in a dark color
- Sewing needle and pins
- Small embroidery hoop

MEASURING UP

Traditionally, rectangular tablemats measure approximately 8 in × 12 in (20 cm × 30 cm), but they are often larger in the USA, approximately 12 in × 18 in (30 cm × 45 cm). To decide on the best size for your table, lay out a standard place setting of cutlery with two sizes of plate. You may like to include space on the tablemat for a drinking glass, as here, or you may prefer to place it at the edge of the mat.

Measure the area used and add 1 in (2.5 cm) all round for the hem allowance, plus a little extra to allow the fabric to be mounted easily in the hoop.

Napkins are usually square, varying in size from small tea napkins of 12 in (30 cm) square to large dinner napkins of 24 in (60 cm) square. However, a good all-purpose size for a napkin is 15 in (38 cm) square.

PREPARING THE FABRIC

TABLEMAT

Tack two parallel guidelines to mark the position of the embroidery. Here, the band of motifs is placed about 1½ in (4 cm) in from the finished edge and the band itself is worked over 36 woven blocks of fabric. Extend the band right up to the finished edge on the two long sides, as shown.

NAPKIN

Mark the position of the motif with tacking. Keep it approximately 2 in (5 cm) in from the finished edges.

WORKING THE EMBROIDERY

TABLEMAT

Mount the fabric in the embroidery hoop (page 160) and begin stitching at the centre of the two tacked lines. Work in cross stitch (page 164) and back stitch (page 164) from the chart, using three strands of thread in the needle throughout. Each square on the chart represents one cross stitch worked over two vertical and two horizontal woven blocks of fabric and the lines represent back stitch worked over two blocks.

NAPKIN

Mount the fabric in the embroidery hoop and work the design in cross stitch and back stitch from the chart, using three strands of thread in the needle throughout. Take care to keep the back of the stitching neat and finish off the thread ends securely.

MAKING UP THE PLACE SETTING

1 Press the embroidery lightly on the wrong side with a warm iron, taking care not to crush the stitches. Cut away any surplus fabric round the tablemat, leaving a margin of 1 in (2.5 cm) for the hem allowance.

2 Pin and tack a narrow double hem (page 169) round the edge, turning in the corners neatly. Secure with hand hemming (page 168) or machine stitching.

EACH SQUARE ON the chart represents one cross stitch worked over two vertical and two horizontal woven blocks of fabric, and the lines represent back stitch worked over two fabric blocks.

FLOWERS AND leaves are popular decorative elements throughout the Balkan countries. Here, the border has been worked in bright colors instead of the traditional colors of red thread on a white or natural background.

REPEAT

| 307 | 600 | 796 | 701 |

EASTERN EUROPEAN
PEASANT BORDERS

Embroider this colorful border of birds, flowers and hearts around the hem of a simple, gathered skirt. Accentuate the Eastern European feel of brightly colored embroidery combined with woven braids by adding a crisp, white lace edging peeping out demurely from beneath the hem.

MATERIALS

- Dark green 18 count Ainring evenweave fabric 51 in (130 cm) wide (Zweigart E3793, color 685 Christmas green)
- Selection of woven braids with black backgrounds
- White cotton lace edging
- DMC stranded cotton in the following colors: pink 3609; fuchsia 718; red 666; kingfisher 995; green 907
- Tapestry needle size 24
- Tacking thread in a light color
- Sewing needle and pins
- Dark green and black sewing thread
- Dark green zip
- Hooks and eyes
- Embroidery hoop

MEASURING UP

To make a simple, gathered skirt with a central back seam and zip, first measure your waist and cut out a waistband, making the band deep enough to fold in two lengthways and adding ½ in (1.5 cm) all round for turnings. To calculate the width of your skirt, measure out a rectangle of fabric measuring between two and a half and four times your waist measurement, plus 1 in (2.5 cm) at each end for the seam allowance. Calculate the finished length of your skirt, then add on 4 in (10 cm) for the hem and seam allowance.

PREPARING THE FABRIC

Tack a line along the lower edge of the skirt approximately 3½ in (9 cm) from the raw edge to mark the fold of the hem. Then lay out and tack four or five lengths of braid a few centimetres above this line, keeping each one level with the weave of the fabric. Leave a gap of 38 fabric blocks for the embroidery band which is 32 blocks deep, then tack more braid in position.

WORKING THE EMBROIDERY

1 Mark the centre of the unworked strip along the lower edge of the skirt with a row of tacking stitches running at right angles to the first row of stitches. Mark the centre of the chart with a soft pencil.

2 Mount the fabric in the hoop (page 160), and work the design in cross stitch (page 164) from the chart, using three strands of thread in the needle throughout. Start stitching at the centre of the band and work outwards, remembering that each square on the chart represents one cross stitch worked over two vertical and two horizontal fabric blocks.

3 When reaching the short edges of the fabric, make sure that the two bands of pattern will match when the seam is stitched. This may mean that you have to adjust the fullness of the skirt in order to accommodate complete repeats of the border chart.

MAKING UP THE SKIRT

1 Press the embroidery lightly on the wrong side over a well-padded surface. Use a warm iron and take care not to press too hard and crush the stitching.

2 Machine stitch the braids in position using black sewing thread. Make a plain seam (page 168) at the back of the skirt, leaving an opening to accommodate the zip.

3 Gather (page 171) the top of the skirt, sew in the zip and attach the waistband (page 171). Sew hooks and eyes on to the short edges of the waistband so that it will close neatly when worn.

4 Try on the skirt and turn up the hem allowance along the tacked line, adjusting the length if necessary. Pin and tack an uneven width hem (page 169), then secure with hand hemming (page 168).

5 Slipstitch the lace on to the reverse of the hem so that the shaped edge shows below the hem. Neaten the short edges of the lace and join together with a plain seam (page 168).

CROSS STITCH embroidery makes a bold, colorful statement when combined with patterned braids and contrasted against a dark background fabric. Work the embroidered band outwards from the centre of the skirt, taking care that the ends of the band match at the back when the seam is stitched.

BORDER DESIGNS for cross stitch are very versatile. Use them in single rows to decorate the ends of towels, repeat several to make a deep band across a cushion cover, or embroider one round a tablecloth, using a mirror to help you turn the border neatly at the corners (page 162).

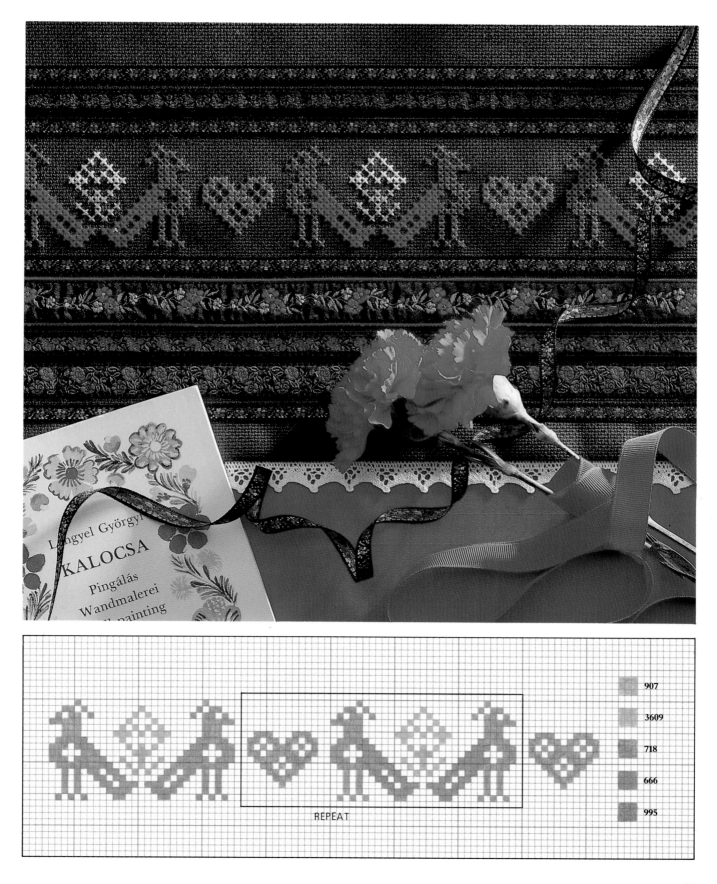

REPEAT

■	907
■	3609
■	718
■	666
■	995

PEASANT BORDERS PATTERN LIBRARY

ROSES PATTERN LIBRARY

HUNGARIAN
ROSES

Hand-cut lead crystal containers show off colorful rose designs inspired by Hungarian folk patterns. Use the decorated jar and bowl to hold sweet-smelling bath salts, talcum powder or tiny individual bars of scented soap and display them in your bathroom.

MATERIALS

- Two pieces 8 in (20 cm) square of white 11 count Pearl Aida evenweave fabric 43in (110 cm) wide (Zweigart E3793, color 1)
- Crystal bowl CT4 and crystal jar CCJ (available from Framecraft, see page 4)
- DMC stranded cotton in the following colors: pinks 603, 3608; reds 349, 600; orange 741; greens 470, 562, 703; blue 791
- Tapestry needles sizes 20 and 24
- Tacking thread in a dark color
- Sewing needle
- Embroidery hoop

PREPARING THE FABRIC

Fold each piece of fabric in four and mark the centre with a few tacking stitches. Mount the fabric in the embroidery hoop (page 160).

WORKING THE EMBROIDERY

1 Work the rose motifs in cross stitch (page 164), starting at the centre of the fabric and working outwards. Use three strands of thread in the size 24 needle and remember that each colored square represents one cross stitch worked over one vertical and one horizontal woven block of fabric.

2 Work the stamens in back stitch (page 164) using two strands of blue thread in the size 24 needle. Finally, work a French knot (page 166) at the end of each stamen using six strands of orange thread in the size 20 needle.

MAKING UP THE BOWL AND JAR LIDS

Press the embroideries lightly on the wrong side with a warm iron, taking care not to crush the stitching. Following the manufacturer's instructions, cut out the embroidered pieces to the correct size and mount them in the silver-plated lids. Secure them in the lids ·by pushing the locking plates firmly into position.

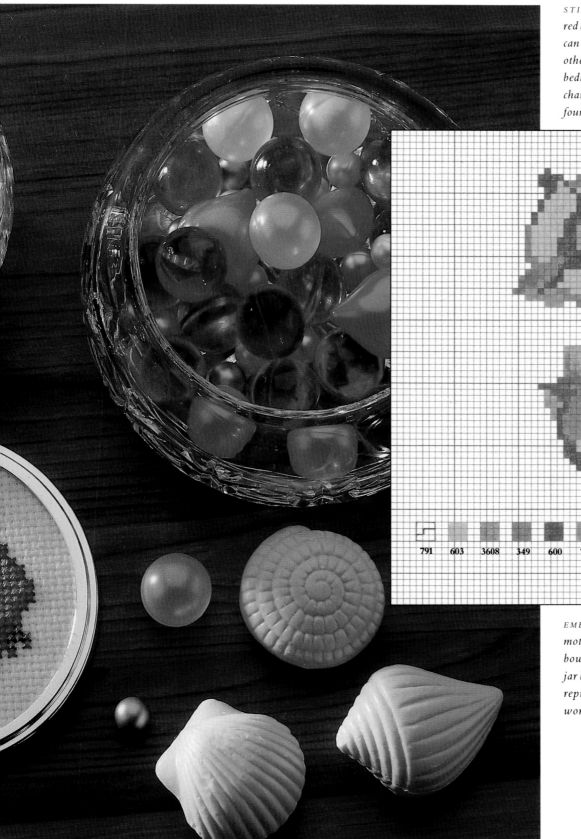

STITCHED IN *shades of pink, red and green, these rose motifs can be used to decorate many other items from bath towels to bedlinen. A further selection of charted Hungarian roses can be found on page 39.*

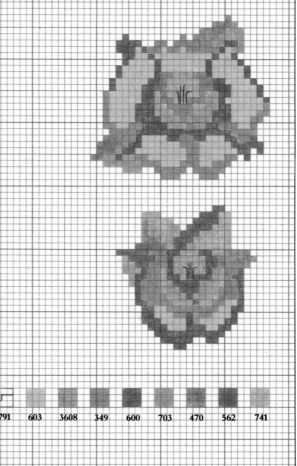

| 791 | 603 | 3608 | 349 | 600 | 703 | 470 | 562 | 741 |

EMBROIDER THE *large rose motif on the lid of the crystal bowl and the smaller one on the jar lid. Each chart square represents one cross stitch worked over one fabric block.*

HEARTS AND FLOWERS

LOVE TOKEN

Hearts and flowers are used extensively on the folk art designs crafted in many of the countries that make up Eastern Europe. What better way to show someone that you care for them than by stitching this love token and giving it to them?

MATERIALS

- Antique white 18 count Ainring evenweave fabric 51 in (130 cm) wide (Zweigart E3793, color 101)
- DMC stranded cotton in the following colors: pink 3607; mauve 553; reds 606, 666, 498, 814; oranges 608, 970; blue 798; greens 906, 909
- Tapestry needle size 24
- Tacking thread in a dark color
- Stitch and tear embroidery backing (optional)
- Sewing needle
- Adjustable rectangular embroidery frame or large embroidery hoop
- Sturdy cardboard
- Strong linen carpet thread or very fine string

MEASURING UP

The embroidered area of the picture covers a rectangle approximately 5¼ in × 4½ in (13.5 cm × 11.5 cm). To this you will need to add at least 4 in (10 cm) all round to allow for mounting the fabric in a frame to work the stitching, and so that the finished embroidery can be laced round a piece of cardboard prior to framing. You may need to add a wider margin of fabric round the edge of the stitched area when working on a rectangular embroidery frame.

PREPARING THE FABRIC

Cut out the fabric and tack a vertical line through the centre of the fabric, taking care not to cross any vertical threads. Mark the central horizontal line in the same way and mark the centre of the chart with a soft pencil. Mount the fabric in the embroidery hoop or frame (page 160). If you are not an experienced stitcher, you may like to tack a piece of stitch and tear embroidery backing on to the wrong side of the fabric. This will give the fabric extra stability while you are stitching and help to prevent puckering.

HERE, A PAINTED wooden frame has been specially made in order to use the love token as a wall decoration, but the embroidery would look equally attractive if you mounted it in a red or pink ready-made greetings card.

EACH COLORED square on the chart represents one cross stitch worked over two vertical and two horizontal fabric blocks. Back stitch is indicated by colored lines on the chart.

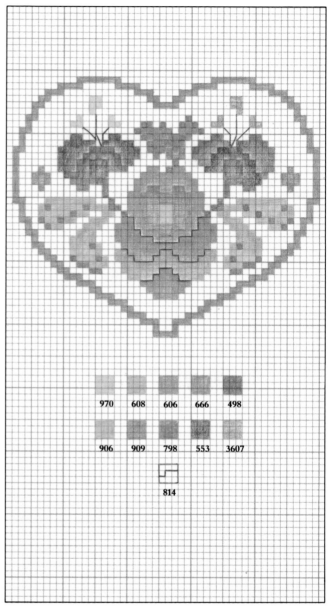

| 970 | 608 | 606 | 666 | 498 |
| 906 | 909 | 798 | 553 | 3607 |

814

WORKING THE EMBROIDERY

1 Begin stitching at the centre of the design, noting that each colored square on the chart represents one complete stitch worked over two vertical and two horizontal woven blocks of fabric. Work in cross stitch (page 164) using three strands of thread in the needle throughout.

2 When the cross stitch areas have been completed, work the linear details in back stitch (page 164) using two strands of thread. Use green 909 for the stamens and red 814 for the petals. Work each back stitch over two blocks of fabric and take care not to pull the stitching and distort the fabric.

FINISHING THE PICTURE

1 When all the embroidery has been completed, carefully tear away the embroidery backing close to the stitching. Press the embroidery lightly on the wrong side over a well-padded surface. Use a warm iron and take care not to press down too hard and crush the stitching.

2 Decide on the size of frame for the picture, and then lace the embroidery (page 173) securely over a piece of sturdy card cut to the appropriate size. Use strong linen carpet thread or very fine string for the lacing. Follow the suggestions given on page 173 for having the picture framed.

CHAPTER THREE

NORTH AMERICA

The countries of the continent of North America, often known as the New World, have absorbed fascinating cultural influences from all four corners of the globe. Native American and Eskimo craft traditions have existed side by side with those brought by settlers from Western and Eastern Europe, Africa and Asia. This melting pot of cultures has produced many craft styles which are now regarded as particularly American, and the designs shown in the chapter reflect some of this diversity.

The two pincushions on page 48 are decorated with the Canadian emblem, a red and white maple leaf. Small-scale projects like these provide the ideal opportunity to try out a new embroidery technique. The smaller pincushion is worked in a traditional way by stitching cross stitch on evenweave fabric, working the background and leaving the motif unworked so that the fabric shows through and becomes an integral part of the design. Here, the maple leaf motif is framed by a deep border outlined in back stitch which appears to have mitred corners. The larger pincushion is executed in an entirely different way as the background is made from canvas rather than evenweave fabric. Here, both the motif and the surrounding area need to be embroidered so that the canvas background is completely covered by the stitching.

The finished embroidery on canvas is framed by a red felt backing, which extends beyond the turned-under edge of the canvas and is cut into neat zigzags using a pair of pinking scissors. The fabric pincushion has a matching fabric backing, to which you could add one or more initials using the alphabet on page 29 or perhaps a short message or greeting using one of the tiny back stitch alphabets on page 65. Other national emblems and flags could be used to decorate a pincushion instead of the maple leaf – simple shapes like stripes and crosses translate easily into cross stitch, while a more complex image such as the Stars and Stripes or the Union Jack would be more difficult to chart.

Decorative Christmas stockings have become an integral part of the present-day American Christmas. They come in all shapes and sizes and are usually decorated with a large, realistic motif with a Christmas theme. Made in pale green evenweave fabric, the stocking shown on page 50 is lined and bound with brightly colored patterned fabric and it has an integral loop so that it can be hung in a suitable spot during the festivities. The stocking is large enough to accommodate the traditional nuts and oranges as well as a net of gilded chocolate coins and several small gifts. The design features a jolly Santa complete with red robe, boots and snowy beard delivering parcels, and the stocking top is decorated with holly and Christmas tree borders and a 'Merry Christmas' greeting. You may prefer to add your own greeting or to personalize the stocking with a child's name. For this reason the alphabet is shown in full on page 29, together with a selection of Christmas motifs. Follow the hints on page 162 to help you space out the letters evenly.

American pieced patchwork quilts are world-famous and old examples of the craft have become very collectable over recent years. Originally thought up by the early settlers as a thrifty method of using up scraps of left-over fabric and of recycling the good parts of worn clothing and household linens, the pieced patchwork quilt has acquired cult status over recent years and many exquisite modern examples of the craft are produced today. Traditional quilt designs have colorful names – robbing Peter to pay Paul, drunkard's path, barn raising, Grandmother's flower garden, morning star, the road to Oklahoma – and special quilts were made as bridal gifts and to commemorate special occasions. Often, several women worked

together on one quilt, piecing the top and then assembling and quilting layers of patchwork, wadding and backing fabric. Each of the women would add their name, the date and sometimes a message for the recipient.

The patchwork design adapted for the cushion cover on page 53 is called log cabin, and it traditionally consists of a symmetrical arrangement of pairs of rectangular strips of patterned fabric. For the cushion cover, the central portion of the design is worked in cross stitch and back stitch, then the embroidery is framed by strips of flower-printed cotton fabric. You can make the cover larger by adding further fabric strips, or by repeating sections of the embroidered design.

The indigenous Native American population of North America produced some of the most original and powerful art across the whole continent. Representing native flora and fauna as well as earth and sky, men and gods, religion and magic, the diversity of Indian art is amazing. The designs varied from tribe to tribe, depending on that people's folklore and tradition, and were applied to clothing and weapons, pottery and baskets as well as jewellery, blankets and beadwork.

The child's denim dungarees on page 56 are decorated with several typically Native American designs, some depicting the thunderbird (a symbol representing the sacred bearer of happiness) and the butterfly (symbolizing everlasting life). Each design is worked separately on dark blue evenweave fabric, then applied to the dungarees with fusible webbing and finally secured with a row of blanket stitch worked round the edge. Further decorated patches can be added to cover worn areas and tears on the dungarees as they occur.

To collect further information about the arts and crafts of North America, look out for pictures of the following: 'Jazz Age' Art Deco designs; Eskimo walrus-ivory carvings and scrimshaw; Deerfield blue and white embroideries; Bargello embroidery; early crewel embroideries from New England; Seminole patchwork; Amish quilts; the traditional patterns of Pennsylvania Dutch decorations; Shaker furniture and furnishings; patterned blankets of the Navaho tribes; Mohave beadwork; Hopi kachina dolls; Apache basketry; decorated 20th-century ceramics by the Keramic Studio; Tiffany lamps and glassware.

NORTH AMERICA is a melting pot of cultural influences from around the world.

MAPLE LEAF
PINCUSHIONS

Two different cross stitch techniques are used to make a pair of pincushions which feature the Canadian national emblem, a red and white maple leaf. The smaller pincushion is stitched on evenweave fabric using a combination of cross stitch and back stitch, while the larger one features the same leaf worked on canvas. The back and front of the fabric pincushion are identical. When making this as a gift you could substitute the recipient's initials for the maple leaf on the reverse.

MATERIALS

- Two small pieces of red 14 count Fine Aida evenweave fabric 43 in (110 cm) wide (Zweigart E3706, color 954 Christmas red)
- Small piece of 17 mesh petit point canvas 23½ in (60 cm) wide (Zweigart E1010)
- Small piece of scarlet felt
- DMC stranded cotton in white
- DMC cotton perlé No. 5 in red 666 and white
- Tapestry needles sizes 22 and 24
- Tacking thread in a light color
- Matching sewing thread
- Sewing needle and pins
- Pinking scissors
- Polyester toy stuffing
- Knitting needle
- Embroidery hoop

MEASURING UP

You will need two pieces of fabric or one each of canvas and felt for each pincushion you make. The finished sizes of the pincushions are as follows: fabric – 3¼ in (8.5 cm) square, canvas – 3½ in (9 cm) square. You will need to add ½ in (1.5 cm) all round to both fabric and canvas pieces for the seam allowance, plus sufficient extra all round to allow you to mount them in the hoop. Add a margin of 1 in (2.5 cm) all round the felt.

PREPARING THE FABRIC

First tack a vertical line through the centre of each piece of fabric or canvas, taking care not to cross any vertical threads. Mark the central horizontal lines with tacking in the same way and mark the centre of the charts with a soft pencil. Mount the fabric in the embroidery hoop (page 160).

WORKING THE EMBROIDERY

FABRIC PINCUSHION

Embroider the design in cross stitch (page 164), working outwards from the centre using two strands of thread and noting that each square on the chart represents one stitch worked over one woven block of fabric. Work the lines shown on the chart in back stitch (page 164), again using two strands of thread in the size 24 needle. Each back stitch is worked over one fabric block. Repeat on the second piece of fabric.

CANVAS PINCUSHION

Work the leaf design in cross stitch (page 164) using cotton perlé in the size 22 needle. Each red square on the chart represents one cross stitch worked over two vertical and two horizontal canvas threads. Fill in the background area with diagonal satin stitch (page 166) using white cotton perlé, then stitch the border in cross stitch with red cotton perlé.

RED AND WHITE threads and fabric are used to stitch a stylized version of Canada's national emblem, the maple leaf. Here, the larger pincushion is worked in cotton perlé on canvas, but you could work this design on evenweave fabric if you prefer.

TAKE CARE TO use the correct chart for the technique you are using. On the fabric chart, the background round the leaf is stitched, allowing the red fabric to remain unworked and make the leaf shape. When working on canvas, you need to stitch both design and background.

MAKING UP THE FABRIC PINCUSHION

1 Press the embroidery lightly on the wrong side with a warm iron. Cut the front and back pieces to the required size, allowing a margin of ½ in (1.5 cm) all round for the seam allowance.

2 Place the front and back pieces together with right sides facing. Pin and tack together, then machine stitch twice round the edge two fabric blocks outside the row of white back stitch with matching thread. Leave a section unstitched along one side.

3 Clip the corners (page 169) and turn the pincushion right side out, taking care to push each corner out gently with the knitting needle. Stuff the pincushion firmly with polyester toy stuffing, using the point of the knitting needle to help manoeuvre stuffing into each corner. Slipstitch (page 168) the opening closed with matching thread.

MAKING UP THE CANVAS PINCUSHION

1 Press the embroidery lightly on the wrong side with a warm iron. If the canvas has become distorted during the stitching, block (page 172) the front. Cut the front to the required size, allowing a margin of ½ in (1.5 cm) all round for the seam allowance.

2 Turn under the seam allowance round the embroidery and tack in place, making sure you turn the corners neatly by cutting away some of the surplus canvas at each corner.

3 Place the front piece on the felt and stitch the two together with red cotton perlé using Holbein stitch (page 164) and leaving a small gap for stuffing the pincushion. Position the row of stitching inside the outer row of red cross stitch.

4 Stuff the pincushion loosely with polyester toy stuffing, using the point of the knitting needle to push the stuffing carefully into each corner. Stitch across the opening and secure the end of the thread neatly. Finally, trim the felt to within ¼ in (5 mm) of the canvas using pinking scissors to make a zigzag edge.

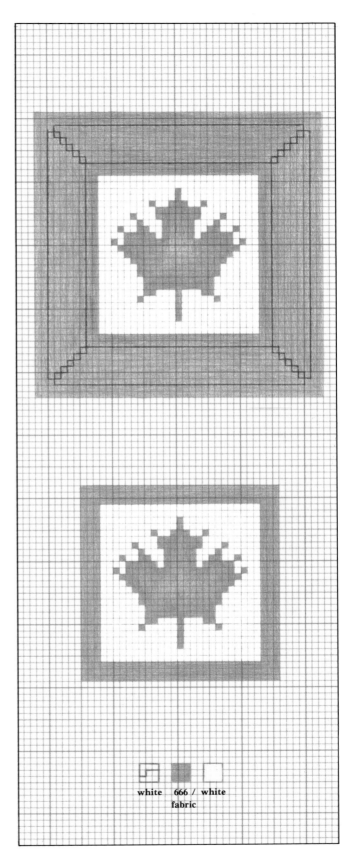

white / white
666 / fabric

AMERICAN
CHRISTMAS STOCKING

Decorated stockings are an important feature of the traditional American Christmas, and the designs often show pictures of Santa Claus delivering presents. A personalized greeting can be substituted for the 'Merry Christmas' shown here.

MATERIALS

- Pale green 11 count Pearl Aida evenweave fabric 43 in (110 cm) wide (Zweigart E1007, color 617 mint)
- Brightly colored cotton fabric for lining
- Red bias binding or printed cotton
- DMC stranded cotton in the following colors: flesh pink 3779; pink 335; mauve 208; reds 606, 666; orange 971; kingfisher 996; blue 3766; greens 702, 910; tans 976, 3776; browns 840, 3021, 3045; greys 415, 3799; white
- Tapestry needle size 24
- Tacking thread in a dark color
- Matching sewing thread
- Sewing needle and pins
- Large embroidery hoop or adjustable rectangular embroidery frame
- Dressmaker's pattern paper

PREPARING THE FABRIC

Make a paper pattern of the Christmas stocking by enlarging the pattern on page 155 and cutting one stocking shape out of dressmaker's paper. Lay the pattern on the evenweave fabric with the toe pointing towards the right and mark the outline on the fabric by tacking round the outside of the paper close to the edge. This is the front of the stocking. Turn the pattern over and repeat for the stocking back. Leave a margin of at least 4 in (10 cm) all round the front to allow you to mount the fabric in the hoop or frame.

Tack a horizontal line across the top of the stocking front approximately 6¼ in (16 cm) from the top edge. This line marks the base of the border. Also mark the centre of this line with tacking. To mark the position of the Santa Claus motif, tack a vertical line down the centre of the tacked shape, taking care not to cross any vertical threads. Mark a horizontal line in the same way, positioning it just above the top of the foot. This marks the centre of the motif. Mark the centre of the motif on the chart with a soft pencil.

WORKING THE EMBROIDERY

1 Mount the fabric in the embroidery hoop or frame (page 160).

2 Work the 'Merry Christmas' border, positioning the bottom edge on the row of tacking across the stocking top and working upwards from the centre. Each square on the chart represents one cross stitch worked over one woven fabric block. Work in cross stitch (page 164) using three strands of thread in the needle, then pick out the holly leaf veins in back stitch (page 164) in three strands of grey 3799. Work each back stitch over one fabric block.

3 Beginning at the centre, work the Santa Claus motif in cross stitch and back stitch in the same way.

MAKING UP THE STOCKING

1 Remove the embroidery from the frame and press lightly on the wrong side over a well-padded surface. Use a warm iron and take care not to crush the stitching.

2 Cut out the embroidered front and the plain back along the tacked lines. Fold the lining fabric with right sides together and cut out two pieces. With wrong sides facing, tack the front to the lining, then repeat for the back.

3 Bind the top raw edges of the tacked shapes (page 170), using ready-made red bias binding or making your own from printed fabric (page 170). Pin and tack the shapes together, with the right sides of the evenweave pieces facing outwards.

4 Bind the remaining raw edges as before, making a hanging loop of binding at the back of the stocking. Remove all tacking stitches.

IF YOU WOULD like to change the 'Merry Christmas' greeting on the stocking, perhaps to personalize it for a child or if you are making it for a friend abroad, use the alphabet on page 29 and follow the guidelines on page 162 to help you space the letters.

A SELECTION of small Christmas motifs is shown in chart form on page 29 and these can be added to the stocking design, perhaps repeated across the top to make a deeper border.

LOG CABIN
CUSHION

American patchwork quilts are famous all over the world and this design is based on one of the best-loved forms, log cabin patchwork, where pairs of matching fabric strips are sewn together in sequence. Here, the design is used on a rectangular cushion, but it can easily be adapted to fit a square cushion pad.

MATERIALS

- Blue 14 count Fine Aida evenweave fabric 43 in (110 cm) wide (Zweigart E3706, color 522 colonial blue)
- Two or more pieces of printed cotton fabric to co-ordinate with the evenweave fabric
- DMC stranded cotton in the following colors: pinks 602, 3708; mauve 554; purple 550; orange 722; pale blue 3747; pale green 504; dark grey 413
- Tapestry needle size 24
- Tacking thread in a dark color
- Matching sewing thread and zip fastener
- Ready-made cushion pad
- Sewing needle and pins
- Large embroidery hoop or adjustable frame

MEASURING UP

The cushion shown here measures 15¾ in × 11¾ in (40 cm × 30 cm) and consists of a central panel of embroidery measuring 10½ in × 7½ in (26.5 cm × 19 cm) framed with strips of coordinating printed fabric in two designs. To adapt the design for a square cushion pad, simply add more strips of printed fabric until you have a cover of the required size.

Decide on the finished size of the cushion cover, bearing in mind that you will need sufficient even-weave and printed fabric to make both the front and back. On the front, add at least 4 in (10 cm) extra all round the embroidered panel to allow you to mount the fabric in your hoop or frame. The back cover is made from two pieces of printed fabric joined by a central seam with a zip fastener inserted, so you will need to add a 2 in (5 cm) seam allowance, plus 1 in (2.5 cm) all round for turnings.

EACH COLORED square on the chart represents one cross stitch worked over two vertical and two horizontal woven blocks. The colored lines indicate rows of back stitch, with each stitch worked over two blocks.

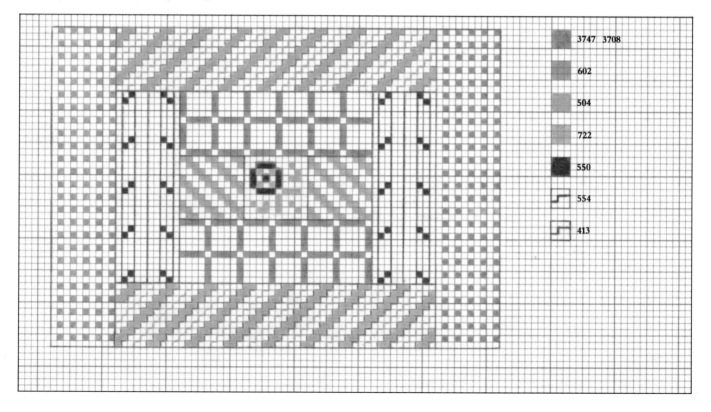

3747	3708
602	
504	
722	
550	
554	
413	

PREPARING THE FABRIC

Cut out the evenweave fabric for the front panel and tack a vertical line through the centre of the fabric, taking care not to cross any vertical threads. Mark the central horizontal line in the same way. Mount the fabric in the embroidery hoop or frame (page 160).

WORKING THE EMBROIDERY

1 Begin working the design in cross stitch (page 164) at the centre of the fabric. Use three strands of thread and note that each colored square on the chart represents one stitch worked over two vertical and two horizontal woven blocks of fabric. When all the crosses are complete, work a St George cross stitch (page 165) over each of the single pale blue crosses in the outer panels, using three strands of pink 3708 thread.

2 Work lines of back stitch (page 164) to correspond with the colored lines on the chart. Work each stitch over two fabric blocks using three strands of the appropriate thread.

MAKING UP THE CUSHION COVER

1 When all the embroidery has been completed, press lightly on the wrong side over a well-padded surface. Use a warm iron and take care not to press too hard and crush the stitching.

2 Cut the printed fabric following the diagram on page 156. Turn under ½ in (1.5 cm) along one long edge of each strip and pin one pair of strips to opposite sides of the embroidered panel, leaving a gap of two unworked blocks between the last row of back stitch and the edge of the printed fabric. Tack and machine stitch in position close to the edge. Repeat with the second pair of strips along the two remaining sides.

3 Follow the illustrated instructions on page 157 for making up the cushion cover.

THE LOG CABIN patchwork effect is created by embroidering six different designs in cross stitch and separating them with rows of dark grey back stitch. The embroidered panel is then framed with printed fabric. If you prefer to embroider the whole cushion front, repeat the charted designs in sequence until the front is filled and omit the printed fabric.

PATCHWORK
PATTERN LIBRARY

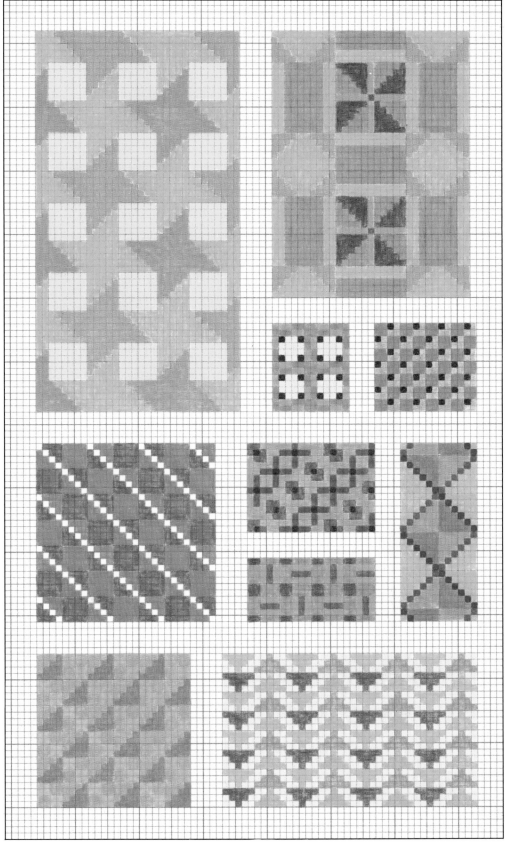

NATIVE AMERICAN
DECORATED DUNGAREES

Embroidered patches featuring designs from Native Americans make a pair of denim dungarees into a very special garment that children will love to wear. The patches are embroidered in cross stitch on patches of evenweave fabric, then applied to the dungarees with rows of blanket stitch.

MATERIALS

- Pair of ready-made denim dungarees
- Small pieces of dark blue 14 count Fine Aida evenweave fabric 43 in (110 cm) wide (Zweigart E3706, color 589 navy)
- DMC stranded cotton in the following colors: orange 350; yellow 444; kingfisher 995; navy blue 823; green 907
- Tapestry needle size 24
- Crewel needle size 8
- Fusible bonding web
- Tacking thread in a dark color
- Sewing needle and pins
- Small embroidery hoop

PREPARING THE FABRIC

The embroidered patches feature single motifs which can be placed anywhere on the dungarees. They can also be worked by the waste canvas technique illustrated on page 163. First tack vertical and horizontal lines on the fabric to correspond with the size of each motif, then fold each piece into four and mark the centres with a pin or a few tacking stitches. Mark the centre of each chart with a soft pencil to give yourself the precise starting point for your stitching.

WORKING THE EMBROIDERY

1 Mount the fabric in the embroidery hoop (page 160), and work the design in cross stitch (page 164) from the chart, using three strands of thread in the needle throughout. Start stitching at the centre of each design and work outwards, remembering that each square on the chart represents one cross stitch worked over two vertical and two horizontal woven blocks of fabric.

2 On the leg patch, work lines of back stitch to correspond with the lines on the chart using three strands of kingfisher thread in the needle. Each back stitch is worked over two fabric blocks.

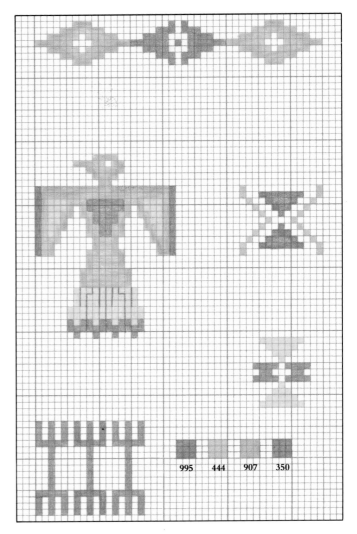

FINISHING THE DUNGAREES

1 Press the embroidery lightly on the wrong side over a well-padded surface. Use a warm iron and take care not to press too hard and crush the stitching.

2 Following the manufacturer's instructions carefully, iron a piece of fusible bonding web on to the back of each embroidery. When the pieces are cool, cut away the surplus fabric round the embroidery, leaving six blocks of fabric round the leg patch and the ankle strip, and four round each of the smaller motifs.

3 Peel away the backing paper from the motifs, position them on the dungarees and press with a steam iron (or ordinary iron and damp cloth) to secure them.

4 Work a row of blanket stitch (page 166) round each patch, using two strands of navy blue thread in the crewel needle. Work the upright stitch over two fabric blocks and space the stitches evenly round the edge, keeping them two blocks apart.

IF YOU DON'T *want to sew embroidered patches on to your dungarees, use the waste canvas technique (page 163) to work the motifs. In this technique, a piece of canvas is tacked on to the fabric to provide a grid for working the stitches neatly and accurately. Each stitch is worked through both the canvas and the fabric, then the canvas threads are removed after all the embroidery has been completed.*

NATIVE AMERICAN *designs are not only colorful, but many of them also have a symbolic meaning, often differing from tribe to tribe. The largest design shown here depicts the thunderbird, known to the Native Americans as the sacred bearer of happiness, while the small ones represent butterflies, the symbol for everlasting life.*

CHAPTER FOUR

LATIN AMERICA

Latin America has a centuries-old tradition of textile crafts and some of the oldest embroideries known to exist have been found on the west coast of South America, many of them dating back to at least the 5th century BC. The three great historic civilizations of the Maya, the Inca and the Aztec have influenced designers throughout the world with their sculpture, intricately shaped and decorated buildings, priceless gold and silver artifacts and strange hieroglyphics. Coupled with a rich diversity of flora and fauna from the lush tropical rain-forests of Brazil to the windswept landscape of Tierra del Fuego, Latin America offers a wide source of images for the embroiderer to interpret.

Butterflies are amongst the most colorful inhabitants of Brazil's endangered tropical rainforests. The charts of the two butterfly pictures on page 62 were adapted from life-size photographs of actual Brazilian species. These butterflies must make a wonderful sight flitting through the forest and at rest, opening and closing their brilliantly colored, iridescent wings. Today, many rainforest species are in decline, with their habitats seriously threatened by forest clear-ances and the consequent soil erosion, together with pollution and chemical damage from man-made pesticides and fertilizers. It would be sad indeed if these wonderful creatures were to dis-appear forever from our world.

Each butterfly chart includes the correct Latin botanical name for each species to add further auth-enticity to your embroidery. There are charts for three more Brazilian species among the designs in the butterfly pattern library on page 65 and these too include their Latin names for you to stitch. You could stitch all five designs on separate pieces of fabric and have each one framed with matching moulding, or alternatively arrange the butterflies into groups of two or three by placing one underneath another in vertical rows. The stranded thread colors have been chosen to match the original photographs as closely as possible, but you may like to substitute a selection of shaded threads for some of the areas or use a strand of blending filament with your threads to add a little sparkle to the design.

Cushion covers are always a popular project with needlewomen as they provide the ideal situation in which to display and use beautiful embroideries. The pair of cushion covers on page 66 feature an elegant geometric pattern inspired by a traditional red, white and blue design decorating the front and yoke of a

Mexican shirt. Cross stitch embroidery is a favourite technique used by Mexican embroiderers and it is often used to decorate garments such as skirts, shirts and trousers. Many Mexican designs are intricate and con-sist of repeating geometric patterns stitched in bright red or blue thread on white fabric.

Here, the two patterns are exactly the same, apart from the color combinations, but the clever use of white and red fabric adds pace and interest to the design. Geometric designs like these look quite complicated and difficult to stitch, but in fact they are relatively straightforward to work providing you always begin stitching at the centre of the design and proceed by working outwards. It is vital to check each group of stitches against the chart as you work, as all the groups must contain the correct number of stitches and

must be placed in exactly the right position on the fabric.

The duffle bag on page 69 is decorated with a band of typical Inca geometric designs taken from the stone carvings which decorated their buildings. The Inca empire flourished during the 15th century, extending from the Peruvian Andes to Ecuador and central Chile, and it had a strong, hierarchical society ruled by an absolute monarch and a complex religion based round the sun god, Inti. The Inca civilization was destroyed by the Spanish in their search for gold during the 16th century, but the remaining artifacts give a valuable insight into this ancient culture. The bag in the photograph is made entirely from evenweave fabric, but you could substitute a hard-wearing cotton drill or denim for the body and base of the bag if you prefer, and use heavy cord for the handle. In this case, work the embroidery on a separate strip of evenweave fabric, turn under the raw edges and machine stitch the strip to the bag before making it up.

Both woven and embroidered textiles produced in Guatemala are brilliantly colorful, and this heritage dates back to the flowering of the ancient Maya civilization during the six centuries from AD 300 to AD 900. This period is regarded as the 'golden age' of Maya culture, when skilled craftsmen constructed great buildings of state, painted pottery and temple walls with bright colors, carved shell, jade and bone into spectacular ornaments and wove the cloth for the humble peasant to wear and to fashion the elaborate costumes of the wealthy.

The Guatemalan people's love of color and bold decoration has remained unbroken right to the present day and the two embroidered brooches on page 72 reflect this delight in color. The brooch designs are embroidered in cross stitch and tent stitch on fine-mesh canvas using bright colors of thread enlivened with areas of white. PVA glue is then spread across the back of each embroidery – this type of glue changes from white to clear as it dries and it is used to secure all the stitches firmly but invisibly in position and so prevent the edges of the embroidery from fraying. A felt backing complete with pin finishes off each brooch.

Further Latin American design sources for you to investigate include the following: ornate plaster, papier mâché and sugar skulls commemorating the Mexican Day of the Dead; the animal kingdom of the tropical rainforest; Aztec mosaics and silverware; pictorial manuscripts including the Codex Mendoza, Codex Nuttall and Codex Florentino; glyphs from the ancient Maya civilization of Central America; Pre-Columbian pottery; Tarabuco weaving from Bolivia; stylized figures of the Inca 'Gold of El Dorado'; decorated cigar boxes and humidors from Cuba; southern Peruvian anthropomorphic figures from the Paracas Cavernas period; carvings and body-painting of the Amazonian Indians.

HISTORIC CIVILIZATIONS and native flora and fauna have exerted an influence on the arts and crafts of Latin America for centuries.

BRAZILIAN
BUTTERFLIES

Brightly colored butterflies abound in the tropical conditions of Brazil's spectacular rainforests. Here, two species are shown, complete with their Latin names. A further selection of Brazilian butterflies is charted on page 65, together with the two back stitch alphabets used for the Latin names.

MATERIALS

- Cream 18 count Ainring evenweave fabric 51 in (130 cm) wide (Zweigart E3793, color 264)
- DMC stranded cotton in the following colors: *Parides ascanius:* pinks 961, 3716, 3779; red 600; yellow 744; tan 922; browns 632, 839, 840; dark grey 3799
  Agrias amydon: purple 333; yellow 973; kingfisher 996; blues 796, 798; greens 3347, 3348; brown 434; dark grey 3799
- Tapestry needle size 24
- Tacking thread in a dark color
- Stitch and tear embroidery backing (optional)
- Sewing needle
- Adjustable rectangular embroidery frame or rectangular wooden stretcher
- Sturdy cardboard
- Strong linen carpet thread or very fine string

MEASURING UP

The embroidered area of the smaller picture (*Agrias amydon*) measures approximately 6 in × 5 in (15 cm × 13 cm), including the border, and the larger picture (*Parides ascanius*) measures 6 in × 5¾ in (15 cm × 14.5 cm), again including the border. To these measurements you will need to add at least 4 in (10 cm) all round to allow for mounting the fabric in a frame to work the stitching, and so that the finished embroidery can be laced round a piece of cardboard prior to framing. You may need to add a wider margin of fabric round the edge when working on a large embroidery frame or on a stretcher which cannot be adjusted.

PREPARING THE FABRIC

Cut out a piece of fabric for each picture and tack a vertical line through the centre of each piece, taking care not to cross any vertical threads. Mark the central horizontal lines in the same way and mark the centre of each chart with a soft pencil. Mount the fabric in an embroidery frame or stretcher (page 161). If you are not an experienced stitcher, you may like to tack a piece of stitch and tear embroidery backing on to the wrong side of the fabric. This will give the fabric extra stability while you are stitching and help to prevent it puckering.

WORKING THE EMBROIDERY

Work each picture in the same way.

1 Begin stitching at the centre of the design, noting that each coloured square on the chart represents one complete stitch worked over two vertical and two horizontal woven blocks of fabric. Work the butterfly design in cross stitch (page 164) using three strands of thread in the needle throughout.

2 Work carefully from the chart, stopping at intervals to check that the top diagonal of each stitch faces in the same direction.

3 Work the Latin name in back stitch (page 164), with French knots (page 166) for the dots. Use two strands of dark grey thread in the needle and work each back stitch over two fabric blocks.

4 Finally, stitch the outside of the name panel and the double border round the butterfly in Holbein stitch (page 164) using two strands of dark grey thread in the needle. Each stitch should cover two fabric blocks.

FINISHING THE PICTURES

1 When all the embroidery has been completed, carefully tear away the embroidery backing (if used) close to the stitching. Press the embroidery lightly on the wrong side over a well-padded surface. Use a warm iron and take care not to press down too hard and crush the stitching.

2 Decide on the size of frame for each picture, and then lace the embroideries (page 173) securely over pieces of sturdy card cut to the appropriate size. Use strong linen carpet thread or very fine string for the lacing.

3 Follow the suggestions given on page 173 for having your picture framed.

STITCH THE butterflies in cross stitch following the charts square-by-square, then work the Latin names in back stitch and French knots. To finish, add the other linear details using Holbein stitch.

PLAIN WOODEN FRAMES show off the delicate shapes and colors of a pair of butterflies from the Brazilian rainforest. Below each butterfly is a panel showing its botanical name.

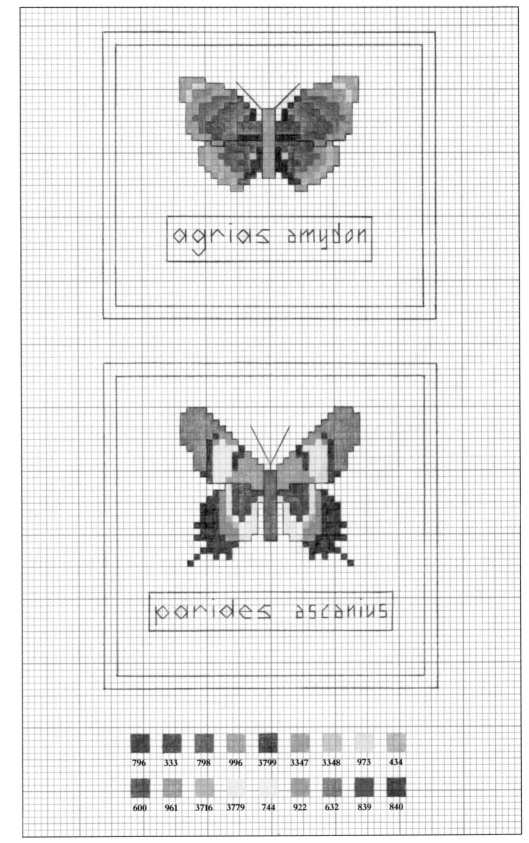

796	333	798	996	3799	3347	3348	973	434
600	961	3716	3779	744	922	632	839	840

BUTTERFLY PATTERN LIBRARY

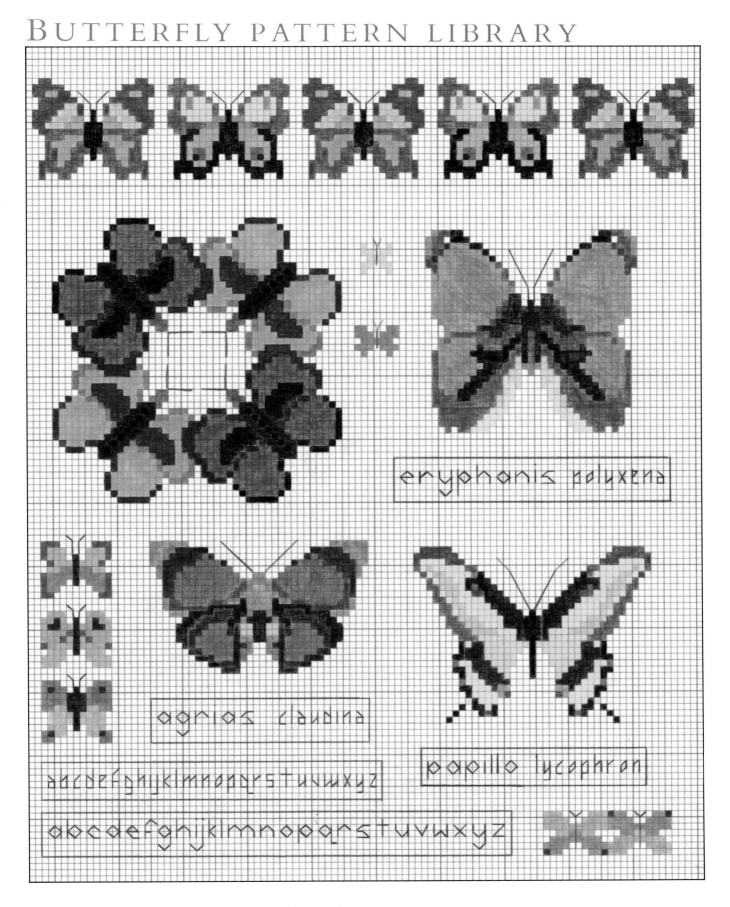

eryphanis polyxena

agrias claudina

papilio lycophron

abcdefghijklmnopqrstuvwxyz

abcdefghijklmnopqrstuvwxyz

MEXICAN
CUSHIONS

The striking geometric pattern featured on this pair of cushions was inspired by a traditional red and white Mexican design. Originally repeated in bands to decorate the yoke of a white cotton shirt, the design is straightforward to work, but you must remember to count the stitches accurately. Always start stitching at the centre of the design and check each group of stitches as they are completed.

MATERIALS

- White and red 18 count Ainring evenweave fabric 51 in (130 cm) wide (Zweigart E3793, colors 101 antique white and 969 Victorian red)
- DMC stranded cotton in the following colors: red 498; blues 791, 796; white
- Tapestry needle size 24
- Tacking thread in light and dark colors
- Matching sewing thread
- Zip fasteners
- Ready-made cushion pads
- Sewing needle and pins
- Large embroidery hoop or adjustable rectangular embroidery frame

MEASURING UP

Decide on the finished size of each cushion cover, bearing in mind that you will need sufficient fabric to make both the front and back. The embroidered area on each cushion front measures approximately 9 in (23 cm) square and each one is surrounded by a border of un-worked fabric approximately 2¾ in (7 cm) deep. On the front, add at least 4 in (10 cm) extra all round to allow you to mount the fabric in your hoop or frame. The plain back of each cover is made in two pieces joined by a central seam with a zip fastener inserted, so you will need to add a 2 in (5 cm) seam allowance, plus 1 in (2.5 cm) all round for turnings.

PREPARING THE FABRIC

Cut out the fabric for the front of each cushion. Tack a vertical line through the centre of the fabric, taking care not to cross any vertical threads. Mark the central horizontal line in the same way and mark the centre of the chart with a soft pencil. Mount the fabric in the embroidery hoop or frame.

THESE CUSHIONS feature the same design worked in alternative colorways of red and blue on white fabric and white and blue on red fabric. The geometric design would look equally effective in other colorways including pale grey and pink on black fabric, or green and blue on cream.

Work each cushion in the same way.

Begin working in cross stitch (page 164) at the centre of the fabric using three strands of thread in the needle throughout. On the chart for the red cushion, the stitched area is indicated in white and blue, while on the white cushion, the stitching is shown as red and blue. Each square on the chart represents one complete stitch worked over two vertical and two horizontal woven blocks of fabric.

Press the embroidery lightly on the wrong side with a warm iron over a well-padded surface. Cut the embroidered front out to the required size, allowing a margin of 1 in (2.5 cm) all round for the seam allowance. Cut out two pieces for the back. Here, the back has been made from matching evenweave fabric, but you can substitute furnishing fabric if you prefer. Follow the illustrated instructions on page 157 for making up the cushion covers.

498 / fabric

791

796

white

ON THE CHART for the red
cushion, the stitched area is
indicated by white and blue
squares, while on the white
cushion, the stitching is shown
in red and blue. Each square on
the chart represents one
complete stitch worked over two
vertical and two horizontal
woven blocks of fabric.

INCA
DUFFLE BAG

Decorate a miniature fabric duffle bag with a geometric border based on Inca designs from the ancient civilization of Peru. The bag closes with a ribbon or cord drawstring and the design is stitched in shades of red, yellow, orange, brown and grey on a khaki background.

MATERIALS

- Khaki 16 count Aida evenweave fabric 43 in (110 cm) wide (Zweigart E3251, color 346 summer khaki)
- Matching cotton fabric for lining
- Matching bias binding
- Orange ribbon or narrow cord for drawstring
- DMC stranded cotton in the following colors: red 816; orange 720; yellow 307; browns 780, 3790; grey 3022
- Tapestry needle size 24
- Tacking thread in a dark color
- Sewing needle and pins
- Matching sewing thread
- 12 brass eyelets (¼ in [5.5 mm] in diameter) complete with fixing tool
- Embroidery hoop or adjustable rectangular frame
- Dressmaker's pattern paper

MEASURING UP

The finished bag measures 9 in (23 cm) deep and 25¾ in (65.5 cm) in circumference. You will need one piece of fabric for the main part of the bag and another piece 8 in × 10 in (20 cm × 25 cm) for the base. You will need to add about 4 in (10 cm) all round the main piece to allow you to mount the fabric in the embroidery hoop or frame.

PREPARING THE FABRIC

Make a paper pattern of the bag by enlarging the diagrams on page 155 to the required size, then cut the main bag piece and the base piece out of dressmaker's paper. Lay the main piece on the right side of the fabric

EACH COLORED square on the chart represents one cross stitch worked over two vertical and two horizontal fabric blocks. Repeat the border right round the circumference of the bag.

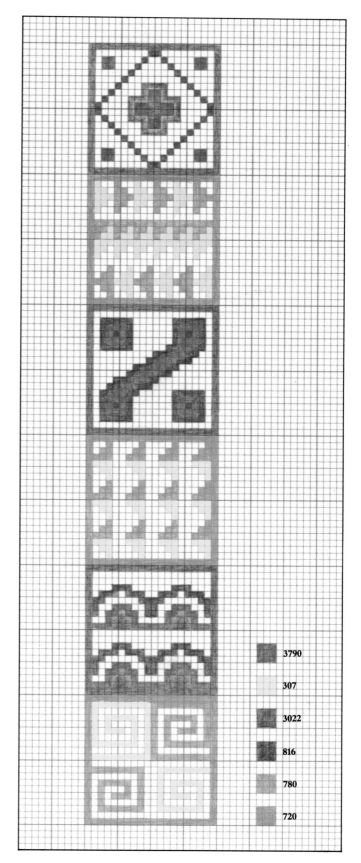

■	3790
▨	307
▨	3022
▮	816
▨	780
▨	720

and tack round the outside close to the edge of the paper. Mark the position of the band of embroidery by tacking a line 1¾ in (4.5 cm) above the lower edge. This line represents the lower edge of the embroidery. Find the centre of the main piece and mark this with a line of tacking at right angles to the first tacked line. Also mark the position of the eyelets on the main piece with tacking. Cut out one base piece from evenweave fabric and two pieces of lining fabric.

WORKING THE EMBROIDERY

1 Draw a line down the centre of the chart with a soft pencil. Mount the fabric in the hoop or frame (page 160).
2 Work the design in cross stitch (page 164) from the chart, using three strands of thread in the needle throughout. Begin at the centre of the band and work outwards, remembering that each square on the chart represents one cross stitch worked over two vertical and two horizontal fabric blocks.

THIS USEFUL BAG closes securely with a drawstring. To make a larger size, simply cut the main piece deeper and work two bands of embroidery round the bag instead of one. See page 71 for more ethnic Inca designs which could be used as alternative decorations for the bag or as the basis for further cross stitch projects.

3 When you reach the end of the chart, repeat the design, working about ½ in (1.5 cm) extra at each side of the band to avoid an unsightly gap in the embroidery when the bag is stitched together.

MAKING UP THE BAG

1 Press the embroidery lightly on the wrong side with a warm iron. Cut away the surplus fabric on the front.
2 Follow the instructions on page 153 for making up and lining the bag.

INCA PATTERN LIBRARY

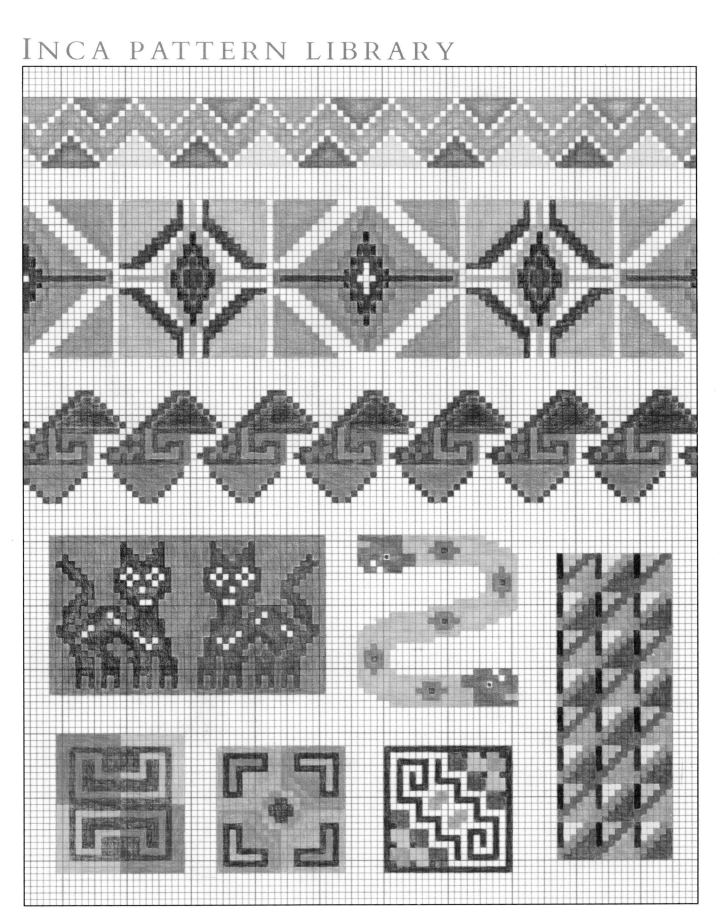

GUATEMALAN
BROOCHES

The jewel-bright colours of Guatemalan woven textiles are reflected in these embroidered brooches. Stitched in a combination of cross stitch and tent stitch on canvas, the brooches are quick and easy to make.

MATERIALS

- Two small pieces of 17 mesh petit point canvas 23½ in (60 cm) wide (Zweigart E1010)
- Scraps of felt in bright colors
- DMC stranded cotton in the following colors: pinks 917, 3608; reds 608, 666; kingfishers 995, 996; turquoise 964; greens 700, 943; white
- Tapestry needle size 22
- Matching sewing thread
- Sewing needle and pins
- White craft glue
- Artist's paintbrush
- Safety pins or sew-on brooch pins

MEASURING UP

You will need one piece of canvas and one piece of felt for each brooch you make. The finished size of each brooch is approximately 1¾ in (42 mm) square. You will need to add a margin of about 1 in (2.5 cm) all round the canvas.

PREPARING THE CANVAS

First tack a vertical line through the centre of each piece of canvas, taking care not to cross any vertical threads. Mark the central horizontal lines in the same way and mark the centre of the charts with a soft pencil. The designs are small enough to be worked directly in the hand without an embroidery hoop or frame, but you should first bind the raw edges with masking tape to prevent the canvas fraying.

WORKING THE EMBROIDERY

Work the design in cross stitch (page 164) from the chart using six strands of cotton in the size 22 needle. Each colored square on the chart represents one cross stitch worked over two vertical and two horizontal canvas threads. Fill in the spaces left unworked with tent stitch (page 166) using six strands of white thread. Work a row of white tent stitch round the brooch, then finish off with a row of pink 3608 or kingfisher 996.

MAKING UP THE BROOCHES

1 Press the embroidery lightly on the wrong side with a warm iron. If the canvas has become distorted during the stitching, block (page 172) each piece.

2 Dilute a little white craft glue with water. Place the brooches face down on a flat surface and carefully coat the backs with white craft glue using the artist's paint-brush, making sure you take the glue right to the edges of the stitching. Allow the glue to dry thoroughly, then repeat with a second coat.

3 Cut away the unworked canvas from round the brooch. Use very sharp scissors and take care not to cut into any stitches. Cut out a felt backing piece the same size as each brooch and stitch a safety pin or brooch back to the centre of the felt. Glue the felt on to the back of the brooch using undiluted white craft glue. Allow to dry thoroughly.

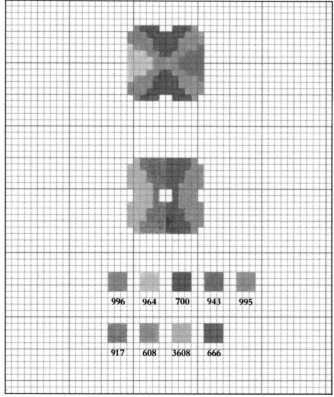

| 996 | 964 | 700 | 943 | 995 |

| 917 | 608 | 3608 | 666 |

CROSS STITCH *and tent stitch are combined on canvas to create a pair of colorful brooches. Small projects like these provide the ideal way of using up any oddments of canvas and thread you may have.*

EACH COLORED *square on the chart represents one cross stitch worked over two vertical and two horizontal canvas threads. After the cross stitch design has been completed, frame the brooch with tent stitch.*

CHAPTER FIVE

AFRICA

The continent of Africa is vast, covering some thirty million square kilometres. This huge area is almost bisected by the equator and is consequently a land of contrasts and contradictions. Two-thirds of the continent has a tropical or subtropical climate and the landscape varies from tropical rainforest, savannah and dry steppes to arid desert and temperate grassland. The decorative arts of Africa reflect these extremes of landscape and climate together with Western European influences imported by Africa's colonists during the last century. Cotton is the most important textile material in Africa, and weaving is an ancient tradition in both western and eastern regions.

The Hausa are an Islamic people from western Africa who decorate their garments with skilfully embroidered patterns of intertwined knots, crescent moons, 'jagged teeth' shapes and circular swirls, the centres of which are filled with intricate stitching. Traditionally, embroidery on Hausa garments is executed by professional male embroiderers who work to commission or sell their wares through local markets. The most elaborately decorated garments are voluminous full-length gowns called rigas. These are worn by men over baggy trousers which are also embroidered. Rigas are huge and are often constructed from three widths of fabric joined together. The fabric is folded over at the top and stitched together along the lower edge, leaving a slit to accommodate the legs. The sides are usually left open for coolness and the front has a large rectangular panel which is heavily embroidered with swirls and the jagged teeth design.

The apron on page 78 is decorated with a typical Hausa intertwined knot motif stitched in the traditional colors of bright red, purple, orange, brown and green. This design can be adapted to suit many other uses. For example, you could work four, six or nine repeats of the intertwined knot chart on evenweave fabric, arranging the knots in a block to make a stunning cushion cover. Alternatively, embroider four repeats in a block (arranged in a one, two and one formation) across the back of a plain dressing-gown or position several repeats in a horizontal row along the lower edge of a gathered evening skirt, working the embroidery using the waste canvas method described on page 163.

Today, African violets are one of the most popular flowering house plants. Growing in the wild only in Tanzania, East Africa, this evergreen species' botanical name is Saintpaulia, in honour of Baron Walter von Saint Paul Illaire (1860–1910) who discovered the first species in the eastern Usambara Mountains. Until the 1970s African violets were notoriously difficult to grow successfully in the home as they were susceptible to overwatering and draughts. Modern hybrids, including miniature and trailing varieties, are much tougher and easier to grow. The delightful blue, violet, pink, red or white flowers are often frilled, striped or splashed with a second colour and, given the right conditions, plants will flower during most of the year. The set of covered buttons on page 80 is decorated with African violet flowerheads and they would add an individual touch to a plain garment cheaply and easily. The flower designs in the photograph are worked on green fabric, but you could substitute a dark color like black or grey instead.

The basketweave napkins on page 82 and the Asante bookmark on page 85 are both small-scale designs suitable for the inexperienced stitcher. Each napkin has a different motif at one corner, and there are eight more small basketweave motifs in the pattern library on page 84, together with a selection of more complicated designs for borders. The bookmark is quick and easy to embroider and it is neatly finished off with a fringe at each end.

The origins of the ornamental beadwork practised in many parts of Africa lie with 15th-century European traders who arrived in Africa with ship-loads of glass beads to trade for gold, ivory and slaves. Coral beads from the Mediterranean and cowrie shells from the Indian Ocean were also bartered for African goods. Beads began to symbolize personal wealth and power, and were applied to many tribal items from life-size figures, thrones and footstools, to crowns, ceremonial gourds and full-length robes.

The Yoruba people of south-west Nigeria have created stunning beadwork items for many centuries to adorn their kings, priests and lesser chiefs. Each king has one or more heavily beaded crowns, ornamented with a hanging, beaded fringe, and his regalia includes other decorative items such as a bead-encrusted robe, staff, footstool and flywhisk. These items are often decorated in relief with grinning faces and birds which contrast with flat areas of zigzags and other geometric patterns. Most Yoruba beadwork is made in a similar way – for example, the crowns have a conical basketwork framework covered with starched cotton cloth. This is ornamented with three-dimensional shapes moulded out of small pieces of cloth dipped in starch. The cotton covering serves as a foundation for thousands of small beads which are strung on thread and tacked in position on the surface of the crown. The two pictures on page 87 were inspired by a group of three-dimensional faces on a piece of Yoruba beadwork. The faces are set in a geometric pattern and you may like to add groups of tiny beads to the faces to make them stand out from the background. Add one bead to every other cross stitch by securing each bead with the top diagonal of the cross. You can find more African beadwork patterns in the pattern library on page 89.

The following sources will provide you with many colorful and unique African designs which can be adapted for cross stitch embroidery: decorated ostrich eggs of the San peoples of the Kalahari Desert; resist-dyed fabrics from Nigeria; shields and spears of Zulu warriors; gold ornaments of the Asante people of Ghana; Masai blanket weaving in Kenya's Masai Mara; traditional tribal dress and turbans; stylized geometric mural painting of southern Africa; West African woodcarvings; beadwork traditions from across the continent, particularly those of Benin, Zaire, Namibia and the Horn of Africa; Bakuba raffia embroidery; southern Africa's native flowers and plants including species of Lithops, the 'flowering pebbles' or 'living stones'

AFRICAN ARTS and crafts reflect native traditions of carving, weaving, basketry and beadwork tempered by imported European traditions.

HAUSA
APRON

The Hausa people of western Africa embellish their robes with colorful patterns, including an elaborate intertwined knot design. Here, the Hausa knot has been adapted to decorate the pocket of a plain apron.

MATERIALS

- Cream 27 count Linda evenweave fabric 33½ in (85 cm) wide (Zweigart E1235, color 264 ivory)
- DMC stranded cotton in the following colors: purple 333; red 321; orange 740; green 700; brown 975; grey 413
- Tapestry needle size 24
- Tacking thread in a dark color
- Sewing needle and pins
- Matching sewing thread
- Dressmaker's pattern paper
- Embroidery hoop

MEASURING UP

The finished pocket size is 6¼ in × 7 in (16 cm × 17.5 cm), so you will need a rectangle of evenweave fabric of this size, plus at least 4 in (10 cm) extra all round for turnings and for mounting in the embroidery hoop.

PREPARING THE FABRIC

First, enlarge the apron pattern given on page 154 to the desired size and cut a paper pattern out of dressmaker's paper. Following the pattern layout on page 154, lay the paper pattern on your fabric, pin in position and cut out the pieces, making sure you allow the extra margin round the pocket piece as indicated on the pattern. Tack a rectangle 6¼ in × 7 in (16 cm × 17.5 cm) on the pocket to mark out the finished size.

WORKING THE EMBROIDERY

1 Tack a vertical line through the centre of the pocket, then tack the central horizontal line in the same way. Mark the centre of the chart with a soft pencil. Mount the fabric in the hoop (page 160).

2 Beginning in the centre and working outwards, work the intertwined knot design in cross stitch (page 164) from the chart, using three strands of thread in the needle throughout. Each square on the chart represents one cross stitch worked over three vertical and three horizontal fabric threads.

MAKING UP THE APRON

1 Press the embroidery lightly on the wrong side with a warm iron, taking care not to press too hard and crush the stitching. Trim away the surplus fabric.

2 Turn a ¾ in (2 cm) double hem (page 169) along the top of the pocket and machine stitch in place. Turn in the other three raw edges along the tacked lines. Pin and tack the pocket in position on the apron front and machine stitch ¼ in (5 mm) from the edge.

3 Turn in a narrow double hem (page 169) round the lower and side edges of the apron front and machine stitch. Gather (page 171) the top edge and attach to the waistband (page 171).

4 Fold the ties in half lengthways with right sides facing and stitch along the long edges. Re-fold so that the seam is at the centre, then stitch across the ends to make a point. Cut away the surplus fabric round the point, turn right side out and press.

5 Turn in seam allowance round the remaining three sides of the waistband and stitch the ties in place. Fold the waistband over and slipstitch round the edge. Topstitch (page 168) round the waistband ¼ in (5 mm) from the edge. Give the apron a final light press.

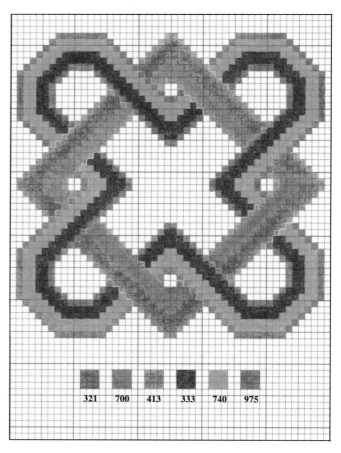

| 321 | 700 | 413 | 333 | 740 | 975 |

HERE, THE APRON *and pocket are made from the same cream evenweave fabric, but you may prefer to make just the pocket from embroidery fabric and apply it to an apron made from inexpensive plain or patterned cotton.*

BEGIN STITCHING *the knot design from the centre of the chart and work outwards, taking care to keep the sequence of interlaced lines correct. Each colored square represents one stitch worked over three vertical and three horizontal fabric threads.*

AFRICAN VIOLET
BUTTONS

Make a set of colorful covered buttons decorated with African violet flowers to liven up a plain jacket or coat. Quick to stitch, the designs are small enough to be worked in the hand without an embroidery hoop. Of course, you can choose different colors to match your garment and your personal preferences.

MATERIALS

- Scraps of green 14 count Fine Aida evenweave fabric (Zweigart E3706, color 670 holly green)
- DMC stranded cotton in the following colors: pink 604; fuchsia 718; purple 552; orange 740; yellow 444; blue 340; black 310; white
- Self-cover button moulds 1¼ in (29 mm) in diameter
- Scraps of green felt
- Fabric glue
- Tapestry needle size 24

MEASURING UP

Draw a circle 2 in (5 cm) in diameter on each scrap of fabric with a dressmaker's pencil. Fold the fabric in four and mark the centre with a pin or a few tacking stitches, then mark the centre of the charts with a soft pencil.

WORKING THE EMBROIDERY

1 Work the designs outwards from the centre in cross stitch (page 164) from the charts using two strands of thread.
2 Outline the petals in back stitch (page 164), using one strand of black thread and following the lines on the charts.

MAKING UP THE BUTTONS

1 Press the embroidered pieces lightly on the wrong side with a warm iron, taking care not to crush the stitches.
2 Cut out circles of felt 1¼ in (29 mm) in diameter and glue one to the top of each mould. Cut out the embroidered fabric round the pencil lines and stretch tightly over the button mould, following the manufacturer's instructions.
3 Attach the button backs, making sure that each design will remain upright when the buttons are sewn on to your garment.

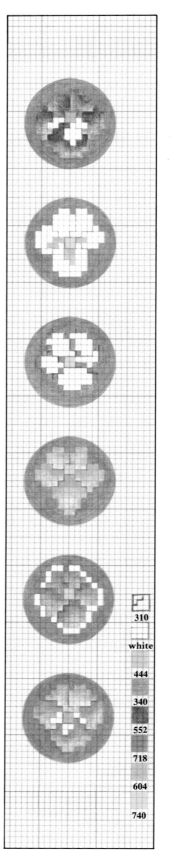

310
white
444
340
552
718
604
740

AFRICAN VIOLET flowerheads decorate a set of self-cover buttons. Use other small-scale cross stitch designs in the same way, or work a set of initialled buttons using the small alphabet shown on page 29.

ALL THE VIOLET designs are worked on the same scale and each colored square on the chart represents one cross stitch worked over one woven block of fabric. To make each design larger or smaller, stitch the charts on 11 or 18 count fabric.

BASKETWEAVE
NAPKINS

DECORATE A SET of napkins with different basketweave designs worked in matching colors of thread. Repeating motifs could also be spaced evenly round the edges of a tablecloth to make an attractive border.

Add style to an informal table setting by stitching a set of napkins trimmed with designs inspired by the intricate patterns woven into African baskets. Two designs are shown here, and more basketweave motifs are presented in chart form on page 84.

MATERIALS

- Cream 18 count Ainring evenweave fabric 51 in (130 cm) wide (Zweigart E3793, color 264)
- DMC stranded cotton in the following colors: light tan 977; rust 920; brown 3021
- Tapestry needle size 24
- Tacking thread in a dark color
- Matching sewing thread
- Sewing needle and pins
- Small embroidery hoop

MEASURING UP

Napkins are usually square, varying in size from small tea napkins of 12 in (30 cm) square to large dinner napkins of 24 in (60 cm) square. Decide on a size which will suit you, adding ¾ in (2 cm) all round for the hem allowance. In general, when using this type of evenweave fabric, a good all-purpose size for a napkin is 15 in (38 cm) square. Lengths of 51 in (130 cm) width fabric can be divided evenly for napkins of this size with sufficient left for hem allowances after trimming away the selvedges. From a 35½ in (90 cm) length of fabric, you will be able to cut a set of six napkins.

PREPARING THE FABRIC

Cut the fabric to the required size and mark the position of each motif with vertical and horizontal lines of tacking. Position the motif approximately 1½ in (4 cm) in from the finished edges on two adjacent sides of the napkin.

WORKING THE EMBROIDERY

1 Begin stitching at the edge of the tacked area. Mount the corner of the fabric in the embroidery hoop (page 160), and work in cross stitch (page 164) from the chart, using three strands of thread in the needle throughout. Each square on the chart represents one cross stitch worked over two vertical and two horizontal woven blocks of fabric.

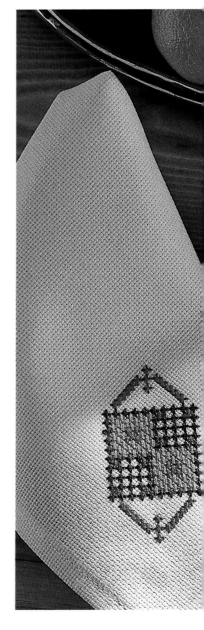

MAKING UP THE NAPKINS

1 Press the embroidery carefully on the wrong side with a warm iron, pressing down lightly and taking care not to crush the stitches.

2 Pin and tack a narrow double hem (page 169) round the edge, turning in the corners neatly. Secure the hem with hemming stitch worked by hand (page 168) or a row of machine stitching using matching thread.

3 For a more decorative edge, work a row of whipped back stitch (page 164) round the hem. Work each back stitch over two fabric blocks using three strands of thread, then whip these stitches with six strands of a contrasting color.

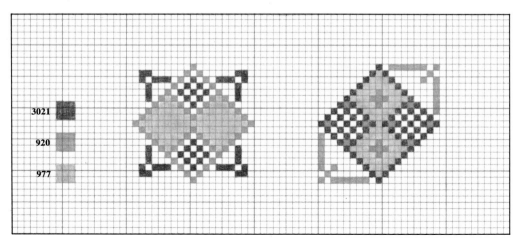

EACH COLORED square shown on the charts represents one cross stitch worked over two vertical and two horizontal woven blocks of fabric.

3021

920

977

BASKETWEAVE PATTERN LIBRARY

ASANTE
BOOKMARK

This design reflects the colorful geometric patterns found on Asante weaving from Ghana. Personalize the bookmark by embroidering a name or set of initials on the reverse, selecting the appropriate letters from the alphabet on page 29.

MATERIALS

- Small piece of cream 11 count Pearl Aida evenweave fabric 43 in (110 cm) wide (Zweigart E1007, color 264)
- DMC stranded cotton in the following colors: red 666; orange 740; blue 798; turquoise 959; cream 712
- Tapestry needle size 24
- Tacking thread in a dark color
- Sewing needle and pins
- Embroidery hoop

MEASURING UP

The finished size of the bookmark is 9 in × 2¼ in (23 cm × 5.5 cm), including the fringe. Here, the embroidery has been worked down the centre of a piece of fabric 5 in (13 cm) wide and then the surplus has been folded over to the back to make an integral lining which neatly covers the wrong side of the stitching. Alternatively, embroider the design on to a narrower strip of fabric and turn in ½ in (1.5 cm) along the side edges. To finish, line the bookmark with a piece of thin cotton or silk fabric in a matching color. Don't forget to add at least 4 in (10 cm) extra all round to allow you to mount the fabric comfortably in the embroidery hoop while stitching.

PREPARING THE FABRIC

Tack a vertical line through the centre of the fabric, taking care not to cross any vertical threads, then tack along the central horizontal line in the same way. Mark the centre of the chart with a soft pencil. Mount the fabric in the embroidery hoop (page 160).

WORKING THE EMBROIDERY

Beginning at the centre of the design, work the design in cross stitch (page 164) from the chart, using three strands of thread in the needle throughout. Each square on the chart represents one cross stitch worked over one fabric block.

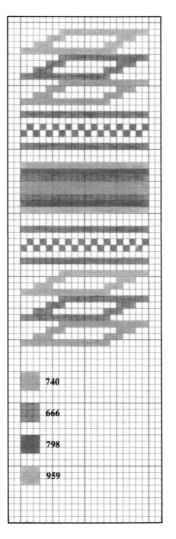

740
666
798
959

EACH SQUARE ON the chart represents one cross stitch worked over one woven block of fabric.

MAKING UP THE BOOKMARK

1 Press the embroidery lightly on the wrong side over a well-padded surface. Use a warm iron and take care not to press too hard and crush the stitching.

2 Cut the fabric to the required size and turn the fabric in along each side edge, leaving a margin of two blocks of unworked fabric. On the back, turn under one raw edge so that the fold overlaps the other raw edge and slipstitch (page 168) in place.

3 Fringe the short edges by carefully teasing away 15 rows of horizontal fabric threads with a tapestry needle, making sure you leave a margin of 10 fabric blocks between the embroidery and the fringing.

4 Secure the side edges with a row of back stitch (page 164) using three strands of cream thread. Work a row of blanket stitch (page 166) along the first row of unfringed fabric at each end of the bookmark, again using three strands of cream thread.

A BOOKMARK IS *the ideal project when you want to use up*
a small, left-over piece of evenweave fabric and oddments
of thread. This design would look equally effective worked in
a color scheme of pastel threads on a dark background.

YORUBA
MASKS

Beads have been used both as currency and personal adornment since the earliest times, and African beadwork shows a wide variety of design styles. The Yoruba people of Nigeria are well known for their beaded robes and three-dimensional figures, and many of their designs feature colorful mask faces set in a background of geometric all-over patterns.

MATERIALS

- Antique white 11 count Pearl Aida evenweave fabric 43 in (110 cm) wide (Zweigart E1007, color 101)
- DMC stranded cotton in the following colors: orange 971; gold 676; dark gold 435; kingfisher blue 996; blue 796; turquoise 959; green 906; tan 922; rust 3777; brown 611; 3787; dark grey 3799; black 310; ecru
- Tapestry needle size 24
- Tacking thread in a dark color
- Stitch and tear embroidery backing (optional)
- Sewing needle
- Adjustable rectangular embroidery frame or rectangular wooden stretcher
- Sturdy cardboard
- Strong linen carpet thread or very fine string

MEASURING UP

The embroidered area of the smaller picture measures approximately 3 in × 4¾ in (8 cm × 12 cm), and the larger picture 4½ in × 6¾ in (11.5 cm × 17 cm). To these measurements you will need to add at least 4 in (10 cm) all round to allow for mounting the fabric in a frame to work the stitching, and so that the finished embroidery can be laced round a piece of cardboard prior to framing. You may need to add a wider margin of fabric round the edge when working on a large embroidery frame or on a stretcher which cannot be adjusted.

PREPARING THE FABRIC

Cut out a piece of fabric for each picture and tack a vertical line through the centre of each piece, taking care not to cross any vertical threads. Mark the central horizontal lines in the same way and mark the centre of each chart with a soft pencil. Mount the fabric in an embroidery frame or stretcher (page 161). If you are

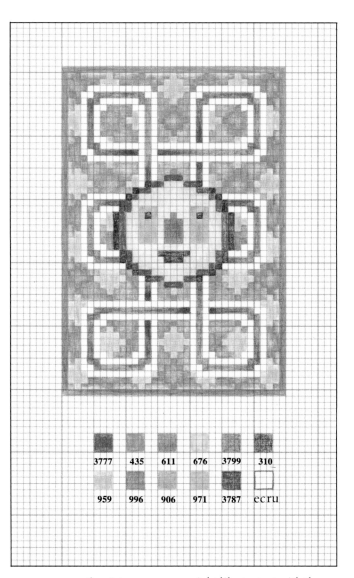

| 3777 | 435 | 611 | 676 | 3799 | 310 |
| 959 | 996 | 906 | 971 | 3787 | ecru |

AS SHOWN IN the picture on page 89, there are two different charts for this project. You *might like to start with the smaller one above.*

not an experienced stitcher, you may like to tack a piece of stitch and tear embroidery backing on to the wrong side of the fabric. This will give the fabric extra stability while you are stitching and help to prevent puckering.

WORKING THE EMBROIDERY

1 Begin stitching at the centre of the design, noting that each colored square on the chart represents one complete stitch worked over one woven block of fabric. Work the design in cross stitch (page 164) using three strands of thread in the needle throughout.

STITCH THE MASKS square-by-square from the chart, making sure that each element is spaced correctly and that the top diagonals of the individual crosses fall in the same direction.

| 310 | 3787 | 435 | 611 | 3777 | 922 | 676 | 971 | 906 | 959 | 996 | 796 | 3799 |

CONTRAST THE brightly colored embroidery with wide, plain frames. Here, the frames are made from copper but a waxed, natural wood surround would look equally good.

2 Work carefully from the chart, stopping at intervals to check that the top diagonal of each stitch faces in the same direction.

3 Outline the edge of each mask in back stitch (page 164) using two strands of dark grey thread in the needle.

FINISHING THE PICTURE

1 When all the embroidery has been completed, carefully tear away the embroidery backing close to the stitching. Press the embroidery lightly on the wrong side over a well-padded surface. Use a warm iron and take care not to press down too hard and crush the stitching.

2 Decide on the size of frame for each picture, and then lace the embroideries (page 173) securely over pieces of sturdy card cut to the appropriate size. Use strong linen carpet thread or very fine string for the lacing.

3 Follow the suggestions given on page 173 for having your picture framed.

AFRICAN BEADWORK
PATTERN LIBRARY

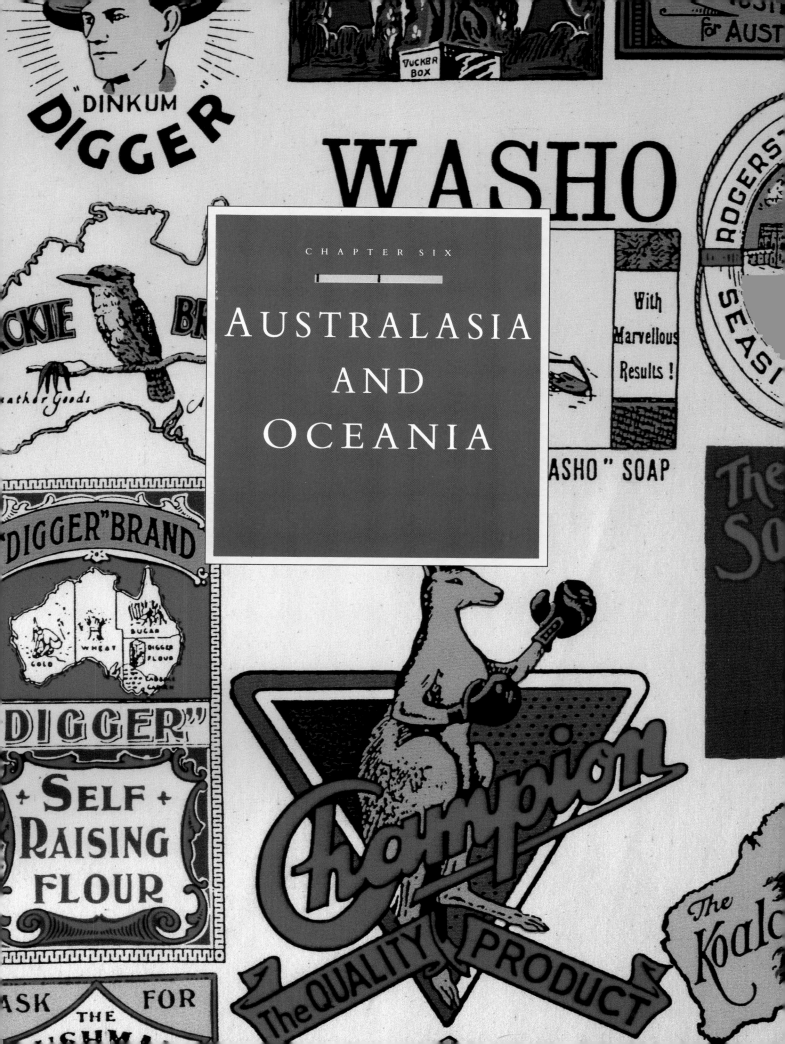

CHAPTER SIX

AUSTRALASIA AND OCEANIA

Australasia and Oceania form a fascinating area which is full of visual contrasts, from picture-postcard views of idyllic, palm-fringed coral islands set in sparkling blue seas, to the lush green forests and rushing waterfalls of New Zealand's Fiordland and the huge uninhabited tracts of land in the Australian outback. A rich tradition of native arts and crafts exists throughout the area, encompassing such features as painted and stencilled barkcloth made on Polynesian islands, Aboriginal paintings and the carved meeting houses of the Maori. Many of the crafts are unique, and nothing like them is found elsewhere in the world.

The outback of Australia is the ancestral home of that country's least privileged people, the native Aborigines. Archaeological evidence from burial sites shows that Aborigines have been in continuous occupation of many parts of the outback for over fifty thousand years – native rock paintings at Obiri Rock, to the east of Darwin, have been dated as ten thousand years older than the mighty pyramids of ancient Egypt and certainly pre-date the famous stone age cave paintings at Lascaux in France. When Britain founded its Australian colonies, all native rights to the land were waived and it automatically became Crown property with no compensation. The natives were persecuted by European settlers until their population was reduced in size by over a quarter of a million to a mere seventy thousand in 1930. Today, persecution of the Aborigines has ceased and the population has increased substantially, but their standard of living is still relatively poor and the subject of Aboriginal land rights has become one of the most controversial issues in contemporary Australian life.

Traditional Aboriginal art stems from the concept of the 'Dreaming' which is the foundation of their culture. The Dreaming, also known as the Dreamtime, refers to a time before history when the Aborigines' Ancestral Beings, the Dreamings, were on the earth, forming the landscape and creating all the plants, animals and peoples of the world. Images of these Dreamings and of their travels and experiences form the largest source of imagery in Aboriginal art. The picture on page 94 was designed by combining several Aboriginal designs of living creatures from bark paintings created in the first half of this century with abstract patterns from more recent paintings. The colors were chosen to accentuate the natural, earthy feel of the design and the finished embroidery was framed in a simple, stained wooden frame. A further selection of Aboriginal designs is found on page 97, including more designs of creatures.

The Maori people are thought to have colonized New Zealand some time after AD 750. Originally from Polynesia, the Maori settled 'The Land of the Long White Cloud' and gradually changed their way of life from hunting and fishing to an agricultural system, structured around extended family clans and a strong religion in which the gods were believed to be related to the people. Inter-tribal warfare was common as mana, or spiritual potency, was created by heroic and warlike deeds and even the slightest insult from a neighbouring clan could result in war. The Maori's myths, stories and sung poems cannot be separated from their intensely creative craftwork as the designs express their deep spiritual beliefs.

Maori wood carving was an exclusively male occupation and the carvers decorated canoes and paddles, war-clubs and boxes to hold the bones of dead chiefs as well as roof beams and wall panels in the clan meeting houses. The panels ornamented the walls on both the inside and outside of the meeting houses, with the outside panels having the most striking carvings, usually of ancestral figures which were carved in deep relief and decorated with inset pieces of abalone shell. Many of the carvings feature intricate swirling and twisting lines. The motif decorating each corner of the traycloth on page 98 is based on a piece of carving from a wooden canoe paddle which was originally painted in red and white. Here, the design fits neatly into a corner, but it can be repeated to make a border.

Dotted across the wide expanse of the Pacific Ocean are hundreds of tropical islands making up the three regions of Oceania. These are Polynesia, Melanesia and Micronesia. Most of these islands were created by volcanic activity several centuries ago, and many are coral atolls (low islands made when a coral reef forms round a submerged volcano, enclosing a shallow lagoon) which are surrounded by deep ocean water. Brightly colored fish including clownfish, squirrelfish and soldierfish dash through the water in and out of the coral and sea-horses swim through the weeds in shallow water. Coral sea motifs are featured on the towel on page 100 and also in the pattern library on page 102.

The Polynesians create a cloth which is called tapa by pounding strips of bark from the paper mulberry tree. Tapa is used to make everyday clothing and for heavily decorated garments for ceremonial wear and traditional designs vary from island to island. The bowl lids on page 103 are decorated with a pattern inspired by the stencilled barkcloth of Mothe Island, Fiji, while other Polynesian designs in the pattern library on page 105 reflect designs used in Hawaii and Tahiti.

From the indigenous peoples' tribal traditions to the unspoilt beauties of the natural landscape, flora and fauna of the region, Australasia and Oceania offer up a wide range of decorative possibilities. Begin your search by investigating the following images: the Maori's carved nephrite and bone tiki ornaments and woven Tukutuku panels; Tahiti and Tonga's Gauguinesque floral fabric designs; traditional Maori facial tattoos; coral island birdlife including the magnificent frigate bird; dramatic carved and painted masks of Melanesia and Easter Island's colossal stone statues.

THIS LARGELY tropical region offers many delightful visual surprises from remote coral islands to native Aboriginal art.

ABORIGINAL
CREATURES PICTURE

Native Aboriginal art offers a wealth of images which both delight and astonish the observer. In this picture, a turtle, a crab and two lizards are stitched in subtle shades of brown, pink and orange to match the rich and earthy colors of Australia. More designs on the same theme can be found on page 97.

MATERIALS

- Cream 18 count Ainring evenweave fabric 51 in (130 cm) wide (Zweigart E3793, color 264)
- DMC stranded cotton in the following colors: pinks 3778, 3779; orange 722; gold 3046; dark gold 435; tan 3776; rust 919; browns 611, 840, 3021, 3772, 3787; beige 644; dark beige 647
- Tapestry needle size 24
- Tacking thread in a dark color
- Stitch and tear embroidery backing (optional)
- Sewing needle
- Adjustable rectangular embroidery frame or rectangular wooden stretcher
- Sturdy cardboard
- Strong linen carpet thread or very fine string

MEASURING UP

The embroidered area of the picture measures approximately 9 in × 17¾ in (23 cm × 45 cm). To this you will need to add at least 4 in (10 cm) all round to allow for mounting the fabric in a frame to work the stitching, and so that the finished embroidery can be laced round a piece of cardboard prior to framing. You may need to add a wider margin of fabric round the edge when working on a large embroidery frame or on a stretcher which cannot be adjusted.

PREPARING THE FABRIC

Cut out the fabric and tack a vertical line through the centre of it, taking care not to cross any vertical threads. Mark the central horizontal line with tacking in the same way and mark the centre of the chart with a soft pencil. Mount the fabric in the rectangular embroidery frame or stretcher (page 161). If you are not an experienced stitcher, you may like to tack a piece of stitch and tear embroidery backing on to the wrong side of the fabric. This will give the fabric extra stability while you are stitching and help to prevent puckering.

WORKING THE EMBROIDERY

1 Begin stitching at the centre of the design, noting that each colored square on the chart represents one complete stitch worked over two horizontal and two vertical woven blocks of fabric. Work the solid parts of the turtle, crab and pair of lizards in cross stitch (page 164) using three strands of thread in the needle throughout. Work carefully from the chart, stopping at intervals to check that the stitches are in the correct positions.

2 Next, work the striped background, horizontal bands and vertical borders in cross stitch from the chart, using three strands of thread in the needle throughout. Again, check each section thoroughly for errors as you work.

3 When all the cross stitch areas are completed, add the linear details in back stitch (page 164), using two strands of thread in the needle throughout. Follow the colors as indicated on the chart. Work each stitch over two blocks of fabric, except for the lizards' claws which are single stitches worked over four fabric blocks.

FINISHING THE PICTURE

1 When all the embroidery has been completed, carefully tear away the embroidery backing (if used) close to the stitching. Press the embroidery lightly on the wrong side over a well-padded surface. Use a warm iron and take care not to press down too hard and crush the stitching.

2 Decide on the size of frame for the picture, and then lace the embroidery (page 173) securely over a piece of sturdy card cut to the appropriate size. Use strong linen carpet thread or very fine string for the lacing.

3 Follow the suggestions given on page 173 for having your picture framed.

CONTRAST THE SUBTLE, earthy colors of the embroidery threads with a stained or painted wooden frame. Here, the frame has been designed so that the embroidery stands out and is emphasized.

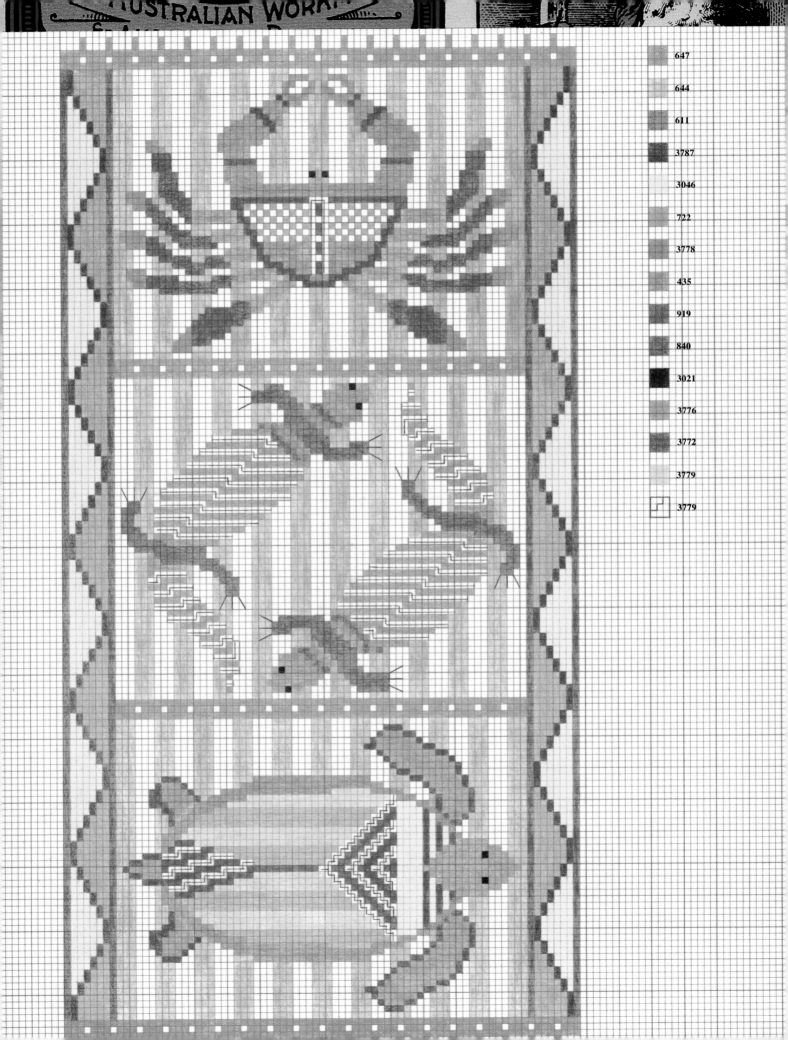

647

644

611

3787

3046

722

3778

435

919

840

3021

3776

3772

3779

3779

ABORIGINAL PATTERN LIBRARY

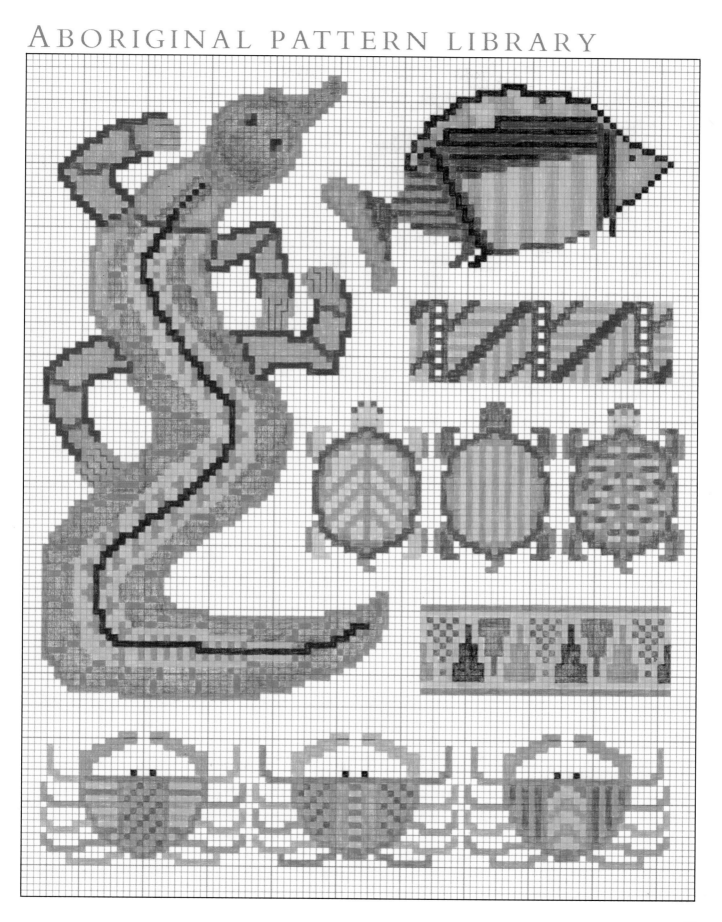

MAORI
TRAYCLOTH

Inspired by the swirling, twisting patterns carved in wood by the Maori of New Zealand, this traycloth features four symmetrical corner motifs. Here, the color of the embroidery thread has been chosen to match the china, but another strong color like dark blue or brown would look equally stylish.

MATERIALS

- Antique white 18 count Ainring evenweave fabric 51 in (130 cm) wide (Zweigart E3793, color 101)
- Narrow cotton lace edging
- DMC stranded cotton in dark red 815
- Tapestry needle size 24
- Tacking thread in a dark color
- Matching sewing thread
- Sewing needle and pins
- Embroidery hoop

MEASURING UP

Measure the length and width of your tray and add at least 4 in (10 cm) extra all round to allow you to mount the design area comfortably in the embroidery hoop while you are stitching. Mark the finished size of the traycloth (excluding lace edging) on the fabric with lines of tacking.

PREPARING THE FABRIC

On the chart, the design covers an area 20 squares wide and 20 squares deep and each colored square represents one stitch worked over two vertical and two horizontal woven blocks of fabric. Before you start to stitch, mark the position of the motifs on the traycloth by marking out an area 40 blocks wide and 40 blocks deep at each corner with lines of tacking. Here, the motifs are placed about 1¼ in (3 cm) from the edge, but you may prefer to move them further in on a large cloth.

WORKING THE EMBROIDERY

1 Tack a vertical line through the centre of each tacked square, taking care not to cross any vertical threads, then tack along the central horizontal line in the same way. Mark the centre of the chart with a soft pencil.

2 Mount the fabric in the embroidery hoop (page 160), and begin stitching the design in cross stitch (page 164) from the chart, using three strands of thread in the

needle throughout. Start stitching at the centre and work outwards, remembering that each square on the chart represents one cross stitch worked over two vertical and two horizontal fabric blocks.

MAKING UP THE TRAYCLOTH

1 Press the embroidery lightly on the wrong side over a well-padded surface. Use a warm iron and take care not to press too hard and crush the stitching.

2 Cut the fabric to the required size, allowing a margin of 1 in (2.5 cm) outside the tacked lines for the hem allowance.

3 Pin and tack a narrow double hem (page 169) round the traycloth, turning in the corners neatly and making sure that the hemline fold runs neatly between two rows of fabric blocks.

4 Tack the lace edging behind the hem, overlapping the raw edges neatly where the ends of the edging meet. To complete the cloth, secure the hem with a row of machine stitching.

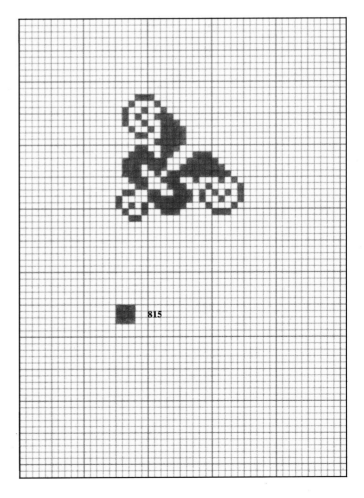

815

MARK OUT THE *shape and position of each corner motif before you begin the embroidery. When decorating a large traycloth, position the motifs further from the edge, or work three motifs at each corner instead of a single one.*

THE CORNER MOTIFS *are simply worked in one color and will suit almost any size of traycloth. Here, they are stitched in dark red on a soft, white fabric, but you can use ecru or a pastel-colored thread on dark fabric if you prefer.*

CORAL SEAS

TOWEL

Decorate plain towels with a pair of delightful sea-horse motifs embroidered on evenweave fabric. Apply one motif to each side of your towel, then finish the whole thing off with a deep band of crochet or heavy cotton lace along one edge.

MATERIALS

- Pale blue 16 count Aida evenweave fabric 43 in (110 cm) wide (Zweigart E3251, color 550 sky)
- Blue or turquoise towel with woven band at each end
- Deep edging of crochet or heavy cotton lace
- DMC stranded cotton in the following colors: pinks 948, 3716, 3779; pale blue 3753; turquoise 3766; greens 320, 772, 966; tan 3776; white
- Tapestry needle size 24
- Crewel needle size 7
- Sewing needle and pins
- Fusible bonding web
- Embroidery hoop

MEASURING UP

Each motif covers an area 3½ in × 10 in (9 cm × 25.5 cm), including the blanket stitch edging. You will need two pieces of fabric at least 4 in (10 cm) larger all round to allow you to mount the fabric comfortably in the hoop.

PREPARING THE FABRIC

First tack vertical and horizontal lines on each piece of evenweave to correspond with the size of the finished motif. Next, fold each piece in four and mark the centre with a pin or a few tacking stitches. Mark the centre of the chart with a soft pencil.

WORKING THE EMBROIDERY

1 Mount the fabric in the embroidery hoop (page 160). Begin working the sea-horse motifs in cross stitch (page 164) from the chart, using three strands of thread in the needle throughout and noting that each square on the chart represents one stitch worked over two vertical and two horizontal woven blocks of fabric.

2 Next, work the outlines in back stitch (page 164), again using three strands of thread and working each stitch over two fabric blocks.

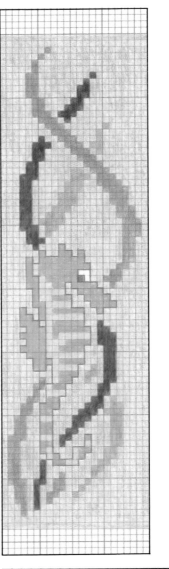
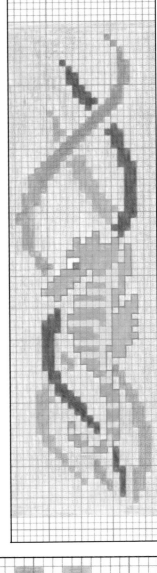

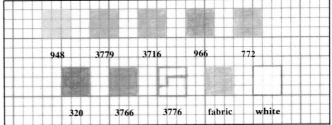

948	3779	3716	966	772
320	3766	3776	fabric	white

EACH COLORED square on the chart represents one cross stitch worked over two vertical and two horizontal woven blocks of fabric. The outlines are worked in back stitch, also over two fabric blocks, using two strands of thread in the needle.

THIS PAIR OF matching sea-horse motifs makes a charming decoration for a bath towel. A charted selection of other fish and shell motifs can be found on page 102, and these can all be used to decorate towels in the same way.

MAKING UP THE TOWEL

1 Press the embroideries lightly on the wrong side over a well-padded surface. Use a warm iron and take care not to press too hard and crush the stitching.

2 Following the manufacturer's instructions carefully, iron a piece of fusible bonding web on to the back of each embroidery. When the fabric is cool, cut away the surplus round the edge, leaving a margin of eight blocks of fabric round the design.

3 Peel away the backing paper from each motif and position one motif at each side of the towel about 5½ in (14 cm) from the base and 1½ in (4 cm) from the side edges. Press with a steam iron (or an ordinary iron and a damp cloth) to secure them.

4 Work a row of blanket stitch (page 166) round each motif, using two strands of the pale blue thread in the crewel needle. Work the upright stitch over two fabric blocks and space the stitches evenly round the edge of the fabric, keeping them two blocks apart and taking care not to pull the stitches too tightly and pucker the fabric.

5 Pin the edging beneath the hem and slipstitch (page 168) it in place with matching thread. If you are using cotton lace rather than a band of crochet to finish off your towel, turn in the raw edges at each end of the edging and hem them (page 168) by hand with matching sewing thread before sewing the edging to the towel. This will ensure that the edges do not fray.

CORAL SEAS PATTERN LIBRARY

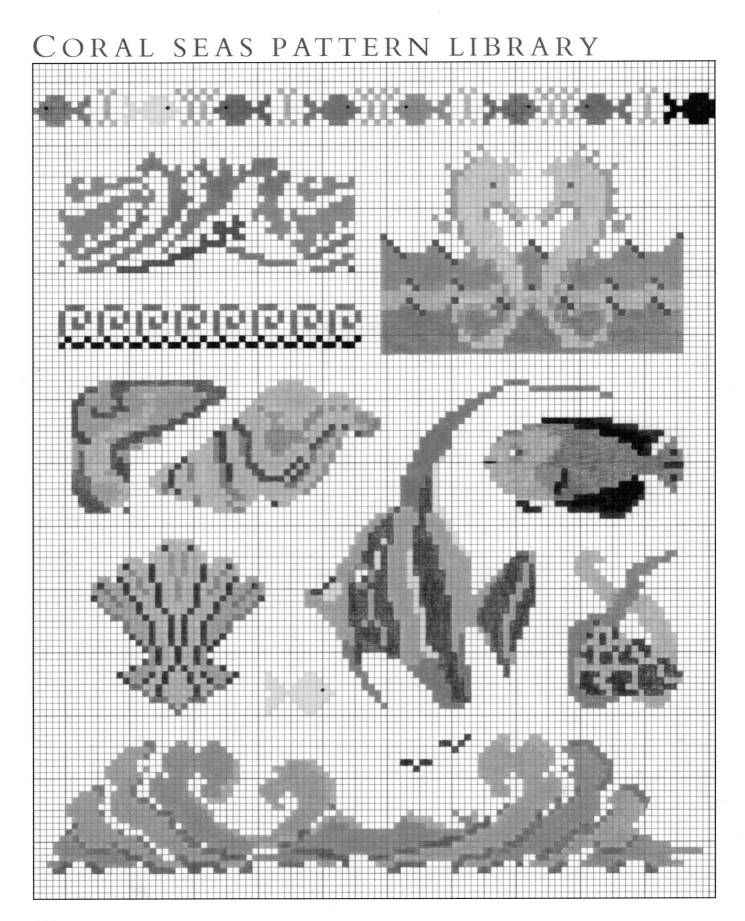

POLYNESIAN
BOWLS

Hand-turned elm bowls make the perfect setting for two simple designs inspired by the stencilled barkcloth created by the Fijians of Mothe Island. Stencilled bark-cloth decoration is only found in this one small area of Oceania and the patterns often feature isolated rosettes or leaf shapes.

MATERIALS

- Small pieces of yellow 11 count Pearl Aida even-weave fabric 43 in (110 cm) wide (Zweigart E1007, color 2 lemon)
- Elm bowls W3E and W4E (available from Frame-craft, see page 4)
- DMC stranded cotton in the following colors: dark red 815; brown 839; dark grey 317
- Tapestry needle size 24
- Tacking thread in a dark color
- Sewing needle
- Embroidery hoop

MEASURING UP

To calculate the size of the fabric pieces, lay the lids on the fabric, then add about 4 in (10 cm) all round for mounting the fabric in the hoop while you are stitching.

PREPARING THE FABRIC

Fold each piece of fabric in four and mark the centre with a few tacking stitches. Mount the fabric in the embroidery hoop (page 160) and mark the centre of the chart with a soft pencil.

WORKING THE EMBROIDERY

Work the motifs in cross stitch (page 164) from the charts, starting at the centre of the fabric and working outwards. Use three strands of thread in the needle and remember that each colored square on the chart represents one cross stitch worked over one vertical and one horizontal woven block of fabric.

MAKING UP THE BOWL LIDS

Press the embroideries lightly on the wrong side with a warm iron. Following the manufacturer's instructions, cut out the embroidered pieces to the correct size and mount them in the lids. Secure the embroideries in the lids by pushing the locking plates firmly into position.

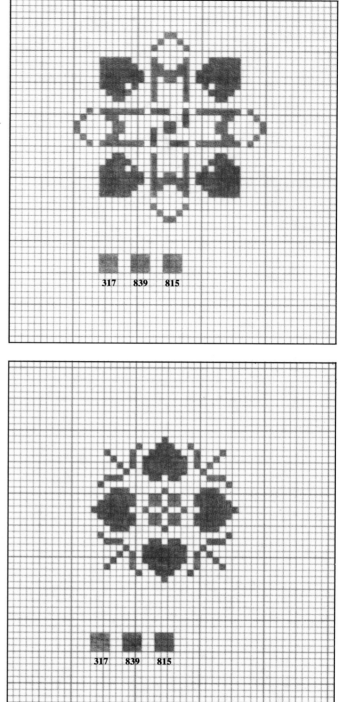

317   839   815

317   839   815

EACH CHART square represents one cross stitch worked over one fabric block. Make sure that you position each motif centrally inside the lid to enhance the symmetry of the designs.

103

STITCHED IN shades of dark red, brown and grey, these rosette motifs are quick and easy to work. *A further selection of charted Polynesian designs is given on page 105.*

POLYNESIAN PATTERN LIBRARY

CHAPTER SEVEN

FAR EAST

The words 'Far East' conjure up a variety of exotic visual images – the 'Mysterious Orient', Chinese New Year celebrations complete with an enormous paper dragon, the exquisitely tragic Madam Butterfly of Puccini's opera, burly Sumo wrestlers, almond-eyed geishas in formal kimonos and obis, Katsushika Hokusai's print 'The Great Wave' from his series of thirty six different views of Mount Fuji, the neon-lit street signs of Hong Kong. The arts and crafts of the Far East have had a great influence on European domestic taste since Western travellers began to visit these far-away lands. This influence reached a peak during the 1920s and 1930s when oriental patterns were in vogue for both fashion and interior decor and even in today's well-travelled society, the Far East exerts a similar fascination.

Lattice designs appear in countries right across the Far East, decorating architecture, textiles, paintings and porcelain with elegant and graceful patterns which manipulate geometric space. The high point of their design occurs in the window lattices on Chinese houses, and these lattices have been regarded as an important folk art for centuries. This art was relatively unknown in the west until Doctor Daniel Dye published his classic 1937 book on the subject, *A Grammar of Chinese Lattice*, after spending over 20 years studying and sketching lattice designs from most parts of China. The designs of window lattices offer an unsurpassed lesson in the variations of related geometric designs from the simple to the intricate, and in the preface to the original edition of his book, Doctor Dye hoped that "these designs and these principles will find gradually a place and an appreciation not only in the Occident but once more in the Orient, and be reincorporated, in a new manifestation, in a new 'wheel-of-life' in the arts and in the materials of the twentieth century".

The lattice photograph frame on page 110 is embroidered on needlepoint canvas. Here, unlike a piece of traditional needlepoint in which the embroidery stitches cover the canvas background completely, areas of unworked canvas are either painted or left their natural yellowish color. This throws the embroidered lattice design into relief to accentuate the oriental feel of the design. The background is painted with acrylic paint as this is hard-wearing and will not flake off the canvas. You may need to use more than one coat of paint to get a

satisfactorily smooth surface on the canvas. Remember to let the painted surface dry thoroughly between each coat and wash your brush in clean water as soon after use as possible. The pattern library on page 112 contains further all-over designs, motifs and borders based on lattices.

The construction of the kimono, the traditional formal costume for Japanese men and women from the 7th century AD, has been simplified by Western designers and it has now become a favourite informal garment. The knee-length kimono on page 113 is decorated with a stylized family crest depicting a paulownia plant and this is worked in cross stitch using the waste canvas technique described on page 163. Japanese family crests represent a

tradition stretching back some 900 years and, within the rigid confines of the circular or square design area, crest motifs have become one of the richest visual traditions in the world.

The crests incorporate a bewildering array of source material and they are thought to represent every plant, animal, bird, fish and natural phenomenon which has existed in Japan throughout the centuries. In addition, there is a wealth of everyday objects, from scissors, sickles, kites and keys to candles, anchors and balls of string. Each separate motif is usually treated in many different ways to produce literally dozens of variations – the motifs are reproduced symmetrically side-by-side, in diamonds, triangles and star-shapes with five or six points, or overlapped, arranged in spirals and sometimes combined with another motif. The pattern libraries on pages 115 and 116 include a further eight designs charted from Japanese family crests.

Chinese characters and symbolism have fascinated Europeans for centuries. The bedlinen on page 117 is decorated with three auspicious symbols – the characters for longevity and double happiness accompany a symbolic representation of the bat, a creature which means both happiness and long life in Chinese mythology. In the traditional blue and white cross stitch embroideries of rural China, symbols for the Five Blessings (longevity, happiness, peace, virtue and wealth) are embroidered on many of the pieces. The symbols are often hidden away in the border or disguised in a large motif.

The pattern library on page 119 contains a Chinese-style Western alphabet which you can use to add your initials or a monogram to your bedlinen. A monogram is composed of two or more letters which are overlapped or interlocked to make a decorative device. To create a monogram from this alphabet, begin by tracing off the first letter on to graphed tracing paper. Position the traced letter close to the next letter, move the tracing paper from side to side until you see a pleasing arrangement and then trace off the second letter. Repeat this procedure to add further letters to the monogram. Stitch the initials or monogram on a rectangle of evenweave fabric and apply this to your article with a row of blanket stitch, or use the waste canvas method to stitch the design on plain fabric.

Sources of Far Eastern designs include the following: Ming Dynasty calligraphy and painting; gold-dragon costume embroidery from the Imperial Chinese courts; 18th-century Chinoiserie designs; delicate famille rose and famille verte porcelain; Samurai arms and armour; Chinese blue and white rural embroideries; prints of the Japanese masters of ukiyo-e, the 'Floating World'; fans, floral printed kimonos, bridges and snow-capped mountains; Japanese lacquerware boxes, rice bowls and chopsticks; the costumes of formal Noh drama, the comic art of Kyogen and the theatre of Kabuki.

THE 'MYSTERIOUS ORIENT'
presents a fascinating combination of
restrained, formal designs and a bold,
imaginative use of color.

LATTICE
PHOTOGRAPH FRAME

Lattice patterns play an important part in the designs of many eastern countries, appearing on textiles, paintings and porcelain. Here, the lattice is worked in cross stitch and diagonal satin stitch on canvas, and the frame contrasts areas of stitched, unworked and painted canvas.

MATERIALS

- 17 mesh petit point canvas 23½ in (60 cm) wide (Zweigart E1010)
- DMC stranded cotton in the following colors: pinks 3607, 3609; red 321; dark red 915
- Tapestry needle size 22
- Tacking thread in a dark color
- Sewing needle
- Rectangular wooden stretcher
- Drawing pins or staplegun
- White craft glue
- Artist's acrylic paint in red and white
- Small artist's paintbrush
- Double-sided tape or glue
- Sturdy cardboard
- Red or dark pink paper the same size as the cardboard
- Strong linen carpet thread or very fine string

MEASURING UP

The embroidered area of the frame measures approximately 9¼ in × 8 in (23.5 cm × 20 cm). To this you will need to add at least 4 in (10 cm) all round to allow for mounting the canvas in a rectangular stretcher to work the stitching, and so that the finished embroidery can be laced round a piece of cardboard prior to framing.

PREPARING THE CANVAS

First tack a vertical line through the centre of the canvas, taking care not to cross any vertical threads. Mark the central horizontal line in the same way and mark the centre of the chart with a soft pencil. Mount the fabric in the rectangular stretcher (page 161).

WORKING THE EMBROIDERY

1 Begin stitching at the centre of the design by working the red lattice in cross stitch (page 164), using six strands of thread in the needle. Each square on the chart colored in red represents one cross stitch worked over two vertical and two horizontal canvas threads.

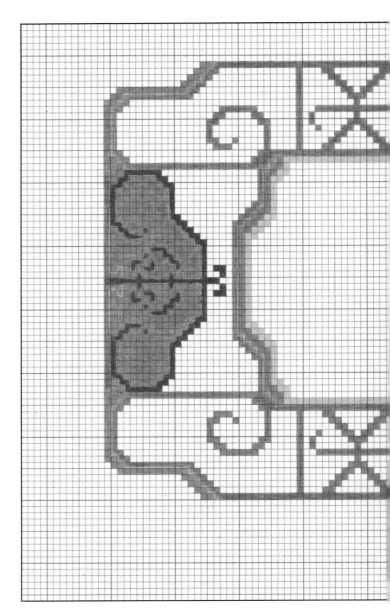

2 When the cross stitch lattice is completed, work the pink portions of the design in diagonal satin stitch (page 166) using six strands of thread in the needle.

FINISHING THE FRAME

1 Press the embroidery lightly on the wrong side with a warm iron while it is still mounted on the stretcher. If the canvas has become distorted during the stitching, remove it carefully from the stretcher and block it (page 172) before replacing on the stretcher for painting.

2 Mix the red and white acrylic paint together until you have a soft, pale pink color. Paint the unworked canvas round the lattice to make a pink border about 1 in (2.5 cm) wide. Allow to dry, then repeat.

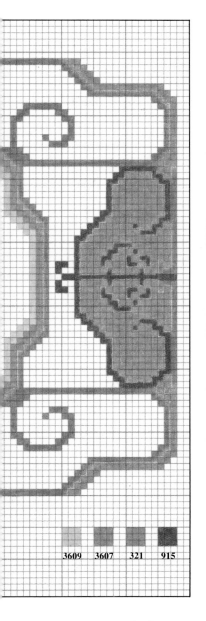

3609   3607   321   915

THE RED areas on the chart represent cross stitch worked over two vertical and two horizontal canvas threads, while the pink areas represent rows of diagonal satin stitch.

THE LATTICE frame makes use of the contrast between heavily stitched areas, unworked canvas and painted canvas. You could substitute pale pink satin stitch for the painted areas.

3 Dilute the white craft glue with a little water and apply carefully to the back of the diagonal satin stitch border round the central area which will be cut away to hold the photograph. Allow to dry thoroughly, then repeat with a second coat.

4 Remove the canvas from the frame. Cut away the central portion of the unworked canvas with a sharp

pair of scissors, taking care not to cut into the stitches. Place the photograph behind the opening and draw round it with a soft pencil. Cut the photograph to the same shape just outside the pencil line, allowing it to overlap the frame slightly. Rub off the pencil lines.

5 Cut a piece of sturdy card to the required size and cover it with the red or dark pink paper. Centre the photograph on the paper and stick it in position with double-sided tape or glue. Finally, lace the embroidery (page 173) securely over the card so that the photograph shows through the opening. Use strong linen carpet thread or very fine string for the lacing and stretch the canvas evenly. Follow the suggestions given on page 173 for having your picture framed.

LATTICE PATTERN LIBRARY

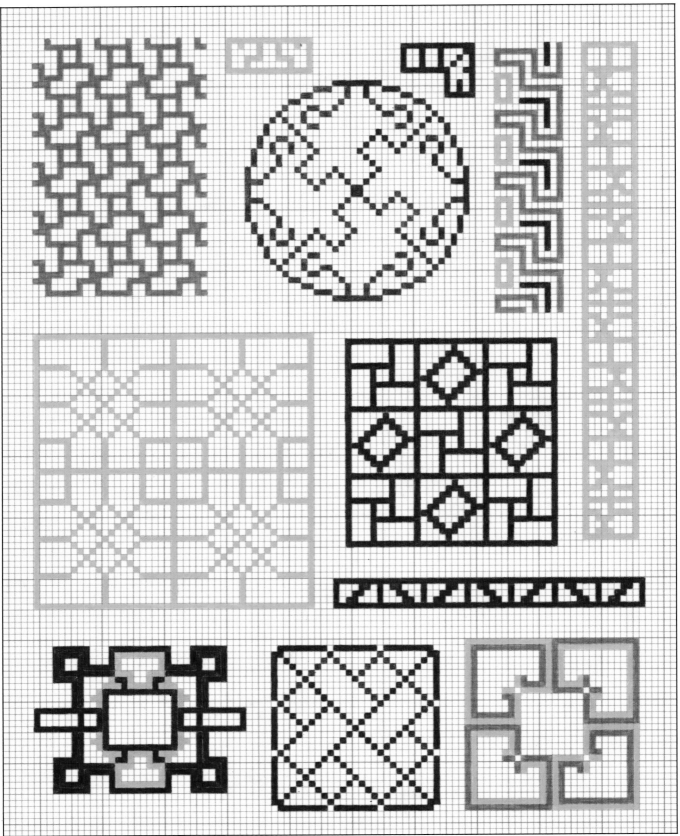

JAPANESE
CRESTED KIMONO

Japanese family crests represent a tradition some 900 years old, and they incorporate practically every plant, animal, bird, natural phenomenon and manufactured object which has existed in Japanese culture through the centuries. Here, a crest showing a paulownia plant has been adapted for cross stitch using the waste canvas technique (page 163) which enables counted thread stitches to be worked neatly on ordinary fabric.

MATERIALS

- Dark blue cotton or polyester/cotton fabric
- Small piece of 8/9 mesh double thread waste canvas 27 in (68 cm) wide (Zweigart E510)
- DMC stranded cotton in orange 970
- Crewel needle size 7
- Tacking thread in a light color
- Sewing needle and pins
- Matching sewing thread
- Embroidery hoop
- Dressmaker's pattern paper

MEASURING UP

Make a paper pattern of the kimono by enlarging the diagrams on page 154 to the required size and cutting the pieces out of dressmaker's paper. Calculate the fabric requirements by following the cutting layout on page 154. Pin the pattern pieces to the fabric according to the layout and cut out the fabric.

PREPARING THE FABRIC

The circular design is positioned in the middle of the back. The design covers an area 38 squares wide and 39 squares deep and each colored square represents one cross stitch worked over one vertical and one horizontal double canvas thread. Count out and cut a rectangle of waste canvas about 10 double threads larger all round than the design. Tack the canvas to the centre of the back piece of fabric, then tack vertical and horizontal lines across the canvas to find the centre. Mark the centre of the chart with a soft pencil.

WORKING THE EMBROIDERY

1 Mount the fabric in the embroidery hoop (page 160), and work the design in cross stitch (page 164) from the chart, using three strands of thread in the needle

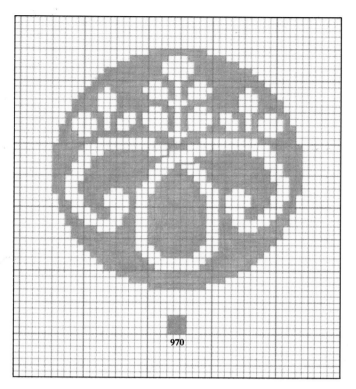

970

FURTHER READY-CHARTED designs inspired by Japanese family crests are given on pages 115 and 116. All these designs can be worked on plain fabric using the waste canvas method, or stitched on evenweave fabric in the usual way.

THIS DESIGN is worked by the waste canvas method, where a piece of canvas is tacked on to plain fabric to provide a grid for working cross stitch neatly and accurately. Each stitch is worked through both the canvas and the fabric, then the canvas threads are removed after all the embroidery has been completed.

throughout. Start stitching at the centre of the design and work outwards, remembering that each square on the chart represents one cross stitch worked over one vertical and one horizontal double thread of canvas.

2 Work the small linear details in back stitch (page 164) using three strands of thread and working each back stitch over one pair of canvas threads.

FINISHING THE KIMONO

1 Press the embroidery lightly on the wrong side over a well-padded surface. Use a warm iron and take care not to press too hard and crush the stitching.

2 Follow the illustrated instructions on page 163 for removing the waste canvas threads.

3 Follow the instructions on page 156 for making up the knee-length kimono.

JAPANESE
PATTERN LIBRARY

JAPANESE
PATTERN LIBRARY

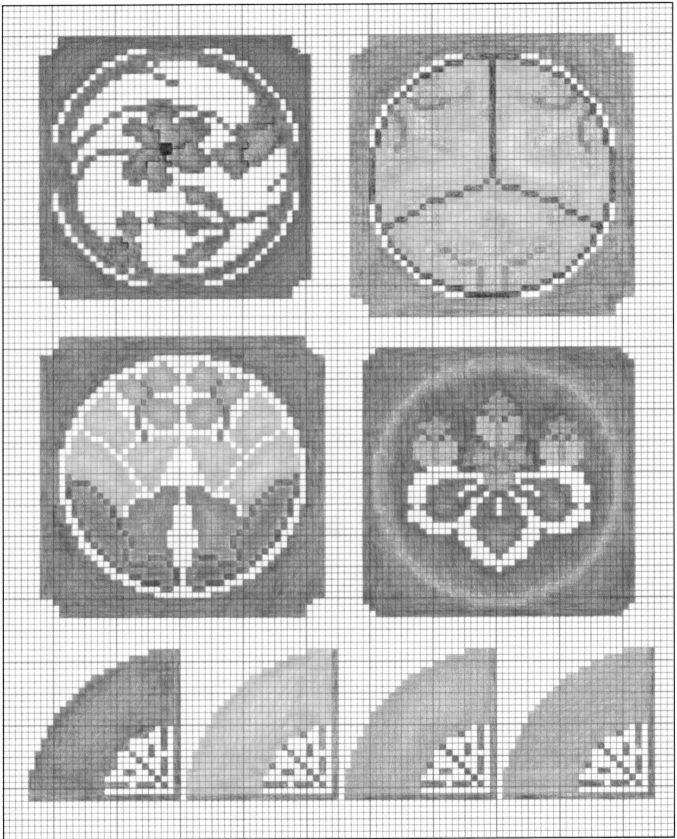

CHINESE

BEDLINEN

Decorate white bedlinen with embroidered patches featuring symbols for longevity and joy, together with the bat of happiness. The patches are embroidered, then applied to the bedlinen with rows of blanket stitch. Alternatively, work the Chinese symbols directly onto the fabric by using the waste canvas technique illustrated on page 163.

MATERIALS

- Ready-made white cotton or cotton/polyester double sheet and a pair of frilled pillowcases
- Scraps of white 11 count Pearl Aida evenweave fabric 43 in (110 cm) wide (Zweigart E1007, color 1)
- DMC stranded cotton in purple 327
- Tapestry needle size 24
- Crewel needle size 8
- Fusible bonding web
- Tacking thread in a dark color
- Sewing needle and pins
- Small embroidery hoop

PREPARING THE FABRIC

The embroidered patches feature single motifs worked separately on evenweave fabric, then applied to the bedlinen with a decorative edging stitch. The stitched motifs are placed at random across the top of the sheet to form a broken band approximately 10 in (25 cm) deep, and two are placed in one corner of each pillowcase, as shown in the photograph. First tack vertical and horizontal lines on the fabric to correspond with the size of each motif, then fold each piece into four and mark the centres with a pin or a few tacking stitches. Mark the centre of each chart with a soft pencil.

WORKING THE EMBROIDERY

Mount the fabric in the embroidery hoop (page 160), and work the design in cross stitch (page 164) from the chart, using three strands of thread in the tapestry needle throughout. Start stitching at the centre of each design and work outwards, remembering that each square on the chart represents one cross stitch worked over one woven block of fabric.

FINISHING THE BEDLINEN

1 Press the embroidered pieces lightly on the wrong side over a well-padded surface. Use a warm iron and take care not to press too hard and crush the stitching.

2 Following the manufacturer's instructions carefully, iron a piece of fusible bonding web on to the back of each embroidered piece. When the pieces are cool, cut away the surplus fabric round the embroidery, leaving a margin of five blocks of fabric round the longevity motif, and four blocks round each of the other two motifs.

3 Peel away the backing paper from the motifs, position them on the bedlinen and press them with a steam iron (or an ordinary iron and a damp cloth) to secure them in place.

4 Work a row of blanket stitch (page 166) round each patch, using two strands of purple thread in the crewel needle. Work the upright stitch over one fabric block and space the stitches evenly round the edge, keeping them one block apart.

THE THREE DESIGNS on the chart represent the Chinese bat of happiness, and symbols for longevity and joy. A Chinese-style alphabet is shown on page 119, and this can be used to personalize your bedlinen.

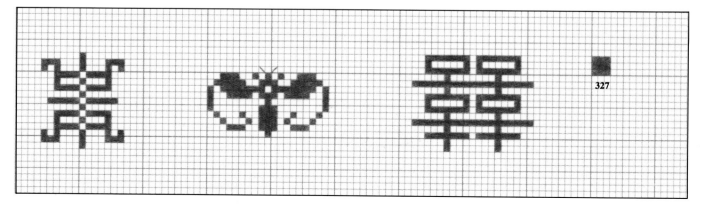

327

IF YOU DON'T *want to sew embroidered patches directly on to the bedlinen, use the waste canvas technique (page 163).*

In this technique, a piece of canvas is tacked on to plain fabric to provide a grid for working the stitches. Each stitch is worked through both canvas and fabric, then the canvas threads are removed after all the embroidery has been completed.

CHINESE PATTERN LIBRARY

CHAPTER EIGHT

MIDDLE EAST

The Middle East is a collective term encompassing the old Ottoman Empire (Turkey and the countries bordering the eastern Mediterranean) and the Arab states stretching from the Caspian Sea to Egypt. The region's two great rivers, the Tigris and the Euphrates, enclose the 'Fertile Crescent', a curving strip of productive land which is kept fertile by moderate rainfall and an extensive irrigation system. In ancient times, three important agricultural communities based in this area grew into the city-kingdoms of Sumer, Babylon and Assyria. Egypt is the site of one of the world's oldest civilizations, the ancient kingdom of the Pharaohs, which was centred around the lush and fertile Nile Delta. The less fertile regions of the Middle East have a harsh climate and this region contains some of the hottest places and the most arid desert lands on earth. The Islamic religion exerts a strong continuing influence on the decorative arts of the entire Middle East, together, of course, with European influences, particularly from Spain, France and Britain.

The slip-on notebook cover on page 124 is decorated with a geometric design inspired by Persian lustre tiles. Ceramic tiles are often used to decorate walls and floors in hot countries as the tiled surface remains cool to the touch, and the combination of blues and greens used in this design adds a cool note to the design.

The superb knotted and woven carpets, saddle blankets and other textiles crafted in the countries of North Africa are among the most beautiful in the world. The patterns and color combinations produced by the weavers are subtle and a delight to the eye. The camel border on page 126 is based on a well-known Gafsa carpet design of a camel caravan, known as a jmel, walking through the desert. Each camel motif is linked into the border by geometric ornaments, and the embroidery is worked in a typically Tunisian color scheme. Use this border design to decorate a gathered skirt or stitch the camel motifs right round a square or rectangular tablecloth, leaving a gap at each corner, then continuing the camel caravan along the adjacent side. The design can also be worked in needlepoint, perhaps in multiple rows to decorate a cushion cover or stool seat, but in this case you will need to embroider the background as well as the camel motifs.

Architecture created during the great civilization of ancient Egypt was monumental in scale and decorated with colorful painted designs of human figures, animals and plants as well as with geometric designs. The lids of the porcelain boxes on page 128 are decorated with stylized lotus and papyrus motifs together with two small-scale geometric designs based on plaited and woven patterns of reeds. The pattern library on page 130 has a selection of border patterns of differing depths featuring designs derived from garlands of flowers, petals, fruit and leaves which were ceremonially buried in tombs and temples.

The Turkish needlecase on page 131 is decorated with a design inspired by the colorful decorated pottery made at Iznik during and after the reign of Süleyman the Magnificent from 1494 to 1566. Iznik pottery decorations, in common with those applied to other decorative arts like metalwork, textiles and wood carving, were heavily influenced by designs for book illustrations and they fall into three categories. First, traditionally stylized leaf and floral scrolls, and secondly the 'saz' style, derived from drawings of an 'enchanted forest', with long, distorted leaves and fantastic flowers. The third category consists of realistic images of garden flowers, leaves and trees. On some pottery, fantastic

'saz' designs rub shoulders with naturalistic sprays of flowers and leaves. The needlecase features an all-over design of stylized leaves and flowers, stitched in one of the traditional Iznik color combinations of blue, greenish turquoise and a strong red.

In ancient Mesopotamia and Egypt, simple geometric principles were applied to architecture, land measurement and astronomical calculations. These principles were developed further by the Greeks, particularly by Euclid who wrote a treatise on geometric rules around 300 BC, and this knowledge had become widely available throughout the Arab world by the end of the 8th century. Geometric principles became increasingly important to the Islamic world as its designs and constructions had deep symbolic and philosophical meanings which were the foundation of the harmony and discipline which characterize all Islamic art. The representation of the human figure was forbidden by the Mohammedan religion and Islam's artistic impulses were translated into geometric patterns and linear designs, often decorated with stylized natural forms and calligraphy.

Islamic geometric designs are based on a system of grids in which identical units are repeated in a regular sequence. The area to be decorated is first broken down into units (squares, hexagons, octagons, eight-pointed stars) of equal size, then an identical geometric figure is drawn inside each unit so that they link up to form a regular grid over the area. The star design featured on page 133 follows these principles, and a further selection of designs based on a star shape is given on page 135.

Visual sources for Middle Eastern designs include the following: symbols and motifs of the ancient art of the city-kingdoms on the Tigris and Euphrates rivers; embroidered Palestinian robes; Jewish decorative traditions; architecture of the Islamic world, particularly minarets, mosques, ogee arches and onion domes; carved lattice-work decorating the doors and balconies of Yemeni palaces in San'a; Turkish textile designs and traditional carpets; the camel-wool weavings and silver jewellery of the nomadic Bedouin of 'Arabia deserta'; rich costume and slipper embroideries of caliphs and sultans from the Arabian Nights; Moroccan rugs and carpets; Islamic calligraphy and manuscripts.

THE ARTS of much of this region are strongly influenced by the Islamic religion with its stylized, geometric patterns.

PERSIAN
TILES NOTEBOOK

Make this embroidered, slip-on cover for a notebook or address book. The design is based on Persian ceramic tiles and is stitched in shades of blue enlivened with turquoise and a bright acid green.

MATERIALS

- Cream 14 count Fine Aida evenweave fabric 43 in (110 cm) wide (Zweigart E3706, color 264)
- DMC stranded cotton in the following colors: blues 341, 518, 796, 798, 823; turquoises 958, 964; green 704; cream 712
- Tapestry needle size 24
- Crewel needle size 7
- Tacking thread in a dark color
- Sewing needle and pins
- Embroidery hoop or adjustable rectangular frame
- Notebook/diary/address book

MEASURING UP

The finished notebook cover measures 5¼ in (13.5 cm) wide and 9 in (23 cm) long. The design can be used to make a cover larger than this by allowing wider fabric margins round the embroidered design. You will need one piece of fabric large enough to wrap round your notebook, plus 1 in (2.5 cm) turnings at top and bottom and 2½ in (6.5 cm) at each side to make the flaps. You will also need to add about 4 in (10 cm) all round to allow you to mount the fabric in the embroidery hoop or frame.

PREPARING THE FABRIC

Fold the fabric in half widthways and mark the centre with a row of tacking. This line marks the centre of the notebook's spine. Wrap the fabric loosely round the notebook, making sure you keep the tacked line centrally down the spine and mark the size of the front of the notebook on to the fabric with rows of tacking. The finished cover is about ¼ in (6 mm) larger all round than the notebook. Find the centre of the tacked rectangle and mark it with a few tacking stitches.

WORKING THE EMBROIDERY

1 Mark the centre of the chart with a soft pencil. Mount the fabric in the hoop or frame (page 160).
2 Work the design in cross stitch (page 164) from the

EACH COLORED square on the chart represents one cross stitch worked over one fabric block. You can vary the size of the cover by leaving a wider margin of unworked fabric round the edge, or by stitching the design on fabric with a smaller count.

THE COVER is made from one piece of fabric and has flaps at each side to accommodate a hard-backed notebook, diary or address book. The edges of the cover are topstitched by hand with a row of back stitch worked in cream to match the fabric.

chart, using three strands of thread in the needle throughout. Begin at the centre of the chart and work outwards, remembering that each square on the chart represents one cross stitch worked over one vertical and one horizontal fabric block.

MAKING UP THE NOTEBOOK

1 Press the embroidery lightly on the wrong side with a warm iron over a well-padded surface, taking care not to press too hard and crush the stitches. Cut away the surplus fabric, leaving top and bottom turnings of 1 in (2.5 cm) and side turnings of 2½ in (6.5 cm).
2 Follow the instructions on page 157 for making up the notebook cover.

964
958
341
798
796
823
518
704

TUNISIAN
CAMELS BORDER

Tunisia is famous for its distinctive hand-made carpets which are characterized by strongly geometric patterns and rich, earthy colors. The camel is a popular carpet motif and this multi-purpose border features a row of stylized camels walking nose-to-tail across the desert.

MATERIALS

- Dull yellow 16 count Aida evenweave fabric 43 in (110 cm) wide (Zweigart E3251, color 237 yellow)
- DMC stranded cotton in the following colors: blue 932; rust 921; browns 612, 3021, 3790; dark grey 3799
- Tapestry needle size 24
- Tacking thread in a dark color
- Sewing needle
- Large embroidery hoop or adjustable rectangular embroidery frame

MEASURING UP

Decide where you would like to use the camel border and calculate your fabric needs accordingly. Details of a simple skirt are on page 36, and those for a cushion cover, traycloth or tablecloth are on pages 66, 98 and 146. The camel border measures 2¾ in (7 cm) deep, and one complete repeat of four camel motifs is 10 in (25 cm) long.

PREPARING THE FABRIC

Begin by tacking a line to mark the position of the base of the border, then mark the centre of this line with a row of tacking. Mark the centre of the chart with a soft pencil to indicate the point at which you should start stitching.

WORKING THE EMBROIDERY

1 Mount the fabric in the embroidery hoop or frame (page 160), and work the design in cross stitch (page 164) from the chart, using three strands of thread in the needle throughout. Start stitching at the centre of the band and work outwards, remembering that each square on the chart represents one cross stitch worked over two vertical and two horizontal fabric blocks.

2 After all the cross stitch has been completed, outline each camel in back stitch (page 164) using two strands of dark grey thread and working each back stitch over two fabric blocks. Finally, work a single dark grey stitch to denote the eye of each camel in the positions indicated on the chart.

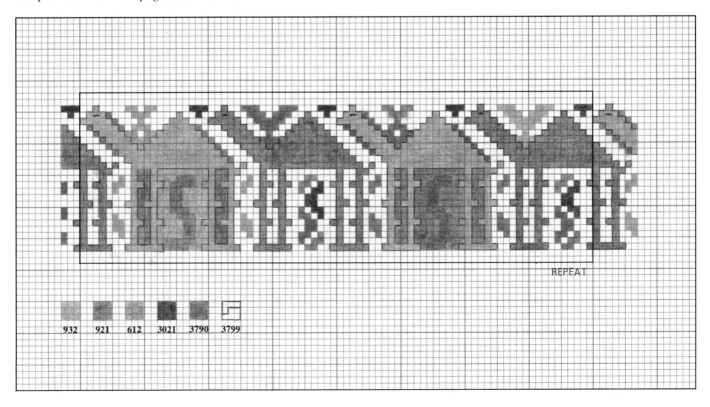

| 932 | 921 | 612 | 3021 | 3790 | 3799 |

EACH COLORED square on the chart represents one cross stitch worked over two horizontal and two vertical fabric blocks. To make the design smaller, work each stitch over single fabric blocks on 14 count fabric. To make it larger, work it over 2 blocks on 11 count fabric.

MAKING UP

1 Remove all tacking stitches.

2 Press the embroidery lightly on the wrong side over a well-padded surface. Use a warm iron and take care not to press down too hard on the embroidery and crush the stitching.

3 Make up your simple skirt, cushion cover, traycloth or tablecloth following the detailed instructions and diagrams supplied on the relevant page.

THE CAMEL border can be used to decorate a simple skirt in the same way as the Eastern European peasant border on page 36, or you could work the design as a border round a rectangular traycloth, turning the corners neatly with the help of a small mirror.

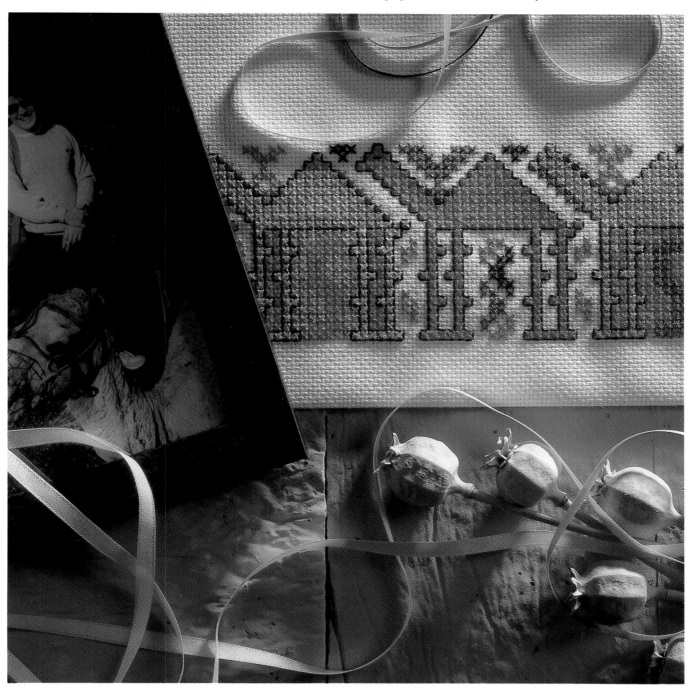

EGYPTIAN
MINIATURES

This set of miniature designs is based on the colorful buildings of the Ancient Egyptians. The completed designs are mounted in the lids of matching black porcelain boxes.

MATERIALS

- Scraps of ivory 14 count Fine Aida evenweave fabric 43 in (110 cm) wide (Zweigart E3706, color 400)
- Porcelain boxes PL1 (small round), PL2 (small oval), PL3 (round) and PL4 (oval) in black (available from Framecraft, see page 4)
- DMC stranded cotton in the following colors: orange 741; gold 783; kingfishers 995, 996; turquoise 958; green 906; tan 3776
- Tapestry needle size 24
- Tacking thread in a dark color
- Sewing needle
- Embroidery hoop

PREPARING THE FABRIC

Fold each piece of fabric in four and mark the centre with a few tacking stitches. Mount the fabric in the embroidery hoop (page 160).

WORKING THE EMBROIDERY

1 Work the motifs and the all-over patterns in cross stitch (page 164), starting at the centre of the fabric and working outwards. Use two strands of the appropriate thread in the needle throughout and remember that each colored square on the chart represents one cross stitch worked over one vertical and one horizontal woven block of fabric.

2 To finish the round and oval boxes, work the linear details indicated on the chart in back stitch (page 164) using two strands of thread and working each stitch over one fabric block.

MAKING UP THE BOX LIDS

1 Press the embroideries lightly on the wrong side with a warm iron over a well-padded surface. Take care not to press too hard and crush the stitches.

2 Following the manufacturer's instructions, cut out the embroidered pieces to the correct size and mount them in the lids. Secure the embroideries in the lids by pushing the locking plates firmly into position.

MINIATURE DESIGNS can be used in a variety of ways. The two geometric all-over patterns shown here would look equally effective stitched on a larger scale to make cushion covers. The other two designs can be used alone, or repeated in rows to make a border round a rectangular tablecloth.

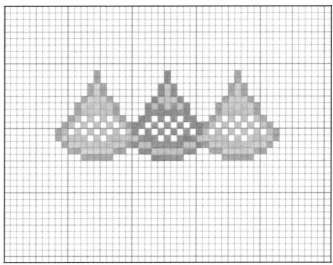

STITCHED IN *shades of
kingfisher blue, green, orange
and tan, the Egyptian designs
can be worked in other color
combinations to suit your decor,
and would look good with a
dark or brightly colored
background fabric. A further
selection of charted Egyptian
designs is given on page 130.*

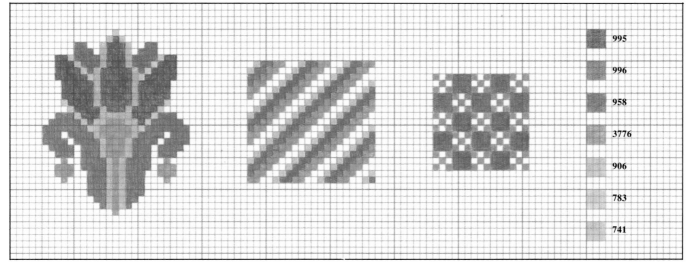

	995
	996
	958
	3776
	906
	783
	741

EGYPTIAN PATTERN LIBRARY

TURKISH
NEEDLECASE

Keep your needles safe and tidy inside this charming circular needlecase. The outside is decorated with an all-over pattern in attractive and vibrant shades of blue, turquoise and deep red based on the traditional decorations of Turkish ceramics, while the inside contains felt leaves large enough to accommodate a wide selection of needles. You can easily draw further inspiration for similar designs from the tiles and mosaics of Turkey with their jewel-bright colors.

MATERIALS

- Yellow 11 count Pearl Aida evenweave fabric 43 in (110 cm) wide (Zweigart E1007, color 2 lemon)
- Contrasting silk or cotton lining
- Lightweight non-woven interfacing
- Two pieces of contrasting felt
- Satin bias binding ½ in (15 mm) wide to match one of the thread colors
- Matching narrow double-sided satin ribbbon
- DMC stranded cotton in the following colors: dark red 816; blue 798, turquoise 959
- Tapestry needle size 24
- Tacking thread in a dark color
- Matching sewing thread
- Sewing needle and pins
- Embroidery hoop
- Dressmaker's pattern paper

MEASURING UP

The finished size of the needlecase (including binding) is 5¾ in (14.5 cm) in diameter. You will need a piece of evenweave fabric 6 in (15 cm) square, with at least 4 in (10 cm) all round to allow you to mount the fabric in the hoop while you are stitching. You will also need a 6 in (15 cm) square of lining fabric and a 6 in (15 cm) square of interfacing.

PREPARING THE FABRIC

Cut a 5¾ in (14.5 cm) diameter circle from dressmaker's pattern paper. Lay this centrally on the evenweave fabric and tack round the outside of the paper. This marks the finished size of the needlecase. Use the paper to help you cut circles of a similar size out of both lining and interfacing. Also cut out two smaller circles in the same way from the felt, using pinking scissors to make a zigzag

edge round each one. Make the first felt circle 4¾ in (12 cm) in diameter, and the second one slightly smaller. Fold the evenweave fabric in four and mark the centre of the tacked circle with a few tacking stitches. Mark the centre of the design on the chart with a soft pencil to indicate the starting point for your stitching and mount the fabric in the embroidery hoop (page 160).

WORKING THE EMBROIDERY

1 Work the all-over design in cross stitch (page 164), starting at the centre and working outwards. Use three strands of thread in the needle throughout and remember that each colored square on the chart represents one cross stitch worked over one vertical and one horizontal woven block of fabric.

2 At the corner of the red-centred squares work a half cross stitch (page 165) radiating outwards. Use three strands of blue thread in the needle.

MAKING UP THE NEEDLECASE

1 Press the embroidery lightly on the wrong side with a warm iron. Take care not to press down too hard and crush the stitching.

2 Carefully cut out the embroidered piece along the tacked outline.

3 Assemble the layers of the needlecase by placing the lining right side down on a flat surface, then laying the interfacing over it, followed by the embroidery with the right side uppermost. Pin and tack the layers together close to the edge. Tack the ribbon ties in position so that one end will be secured under the binding, then bind the edge (page 170) of the needlecase with the satin binding, taking care to fold in the raw edges neatly.

4 Place the two felt circles centrally over the lined side with the smaller circle on top. Secure the layers with a few pins, then turn them over so that the embroidery is facing you. Tack across the centre of the embroidery, making sure you go through all the layers, and take the tacking stitches along one row of holes through the centre of the design.

5 To finish the needlecase, work a row of Holbein stitch (page 164) along the tacked line, taking care to stitch through all the layers so that the Holbein stitches hold the felt circles neatly in position. Finish off the ends of the thread securely, then remove the tacking round the edge and fold the needlecase in half along the line of Holbein stitch. Make a knot at the end of the ribbon ties and tie them in a bow.

EACH COLORED *square on the chart represents one cross stitch worked over one vertical and one horizontal fabric block. The straight stitches at the corners of the square motifs are half cross stitches.*

STITCHED IN *dark red, blue and turquoise, the all-over design can be repeated over a larger area and used to cover a tea-cosy or circular cushion. This design also lends itself to different colorways: dark orange and two shades of green on pale mint green fabric, or three shades of grey on antique white fabric.*

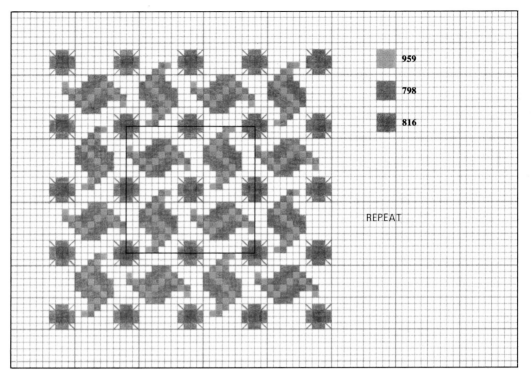

959
798
816

REPEAT

MIDDLE EASTERN
STAR CUSHION

The star motif is a recurring design theme throughout much of the Middle East and its use is as common on textiles and manuscripts as it is both inside and outside buildings. Stitched in vivid colors, this star design would live happily with both modern and traditional furnishing styles. Worked in tapestry wool on canvas, the embroidery is hard-wearing and could easily be used to cover a chair or stool seat.

MATERIALS

- 10 mesh double thread canvas 35½ in (90 cm) wide (Zweigart E1231)
- Furnishing fabric for cushion backing
- Ready-made cushion pad
- DMC tapestry wool in the following colors: purple 7242; red 7157; orange 7947; yellow 7973; blue 7650; green 7915
- Tapestry needle size 20
- Tacking thread in a dark color
- Sewing needle
- Matching sewing thread
- Zip fastener
- Rectangular wooden stretcher
- Drawing pins or staplegun

MEASURING UP

The embroidered area of the cushion shown in the photograph measures 12 in × 10 in (30 cm × 25 cm), but you can make your cushion larger if you wish by simply stitching more of the repeating design. After deciding on the finished size of your cushion cover, add at least 4 in (10 cm) all round to allow for mounting the canvas on a rectangular stretcher to work the stitching. The plain back of each cover is made in two pieces which are joined by a central seam with a zip fastener inserted, so you will need to add a 2 in (5 cm) seam allowance, plus 1 in (2.5 cm) all round for turnings.

PREPARING THE CANVAS

First tack a vertical line through the centre of the canvas, taking care not to cross any vertical threads. Mark the central horizontal line in the same way and then tack a line round the outside of the canvas to denote the finished size. Mark the centre of the chart in pencil. Mount the canvas on the stretcher (page 161).

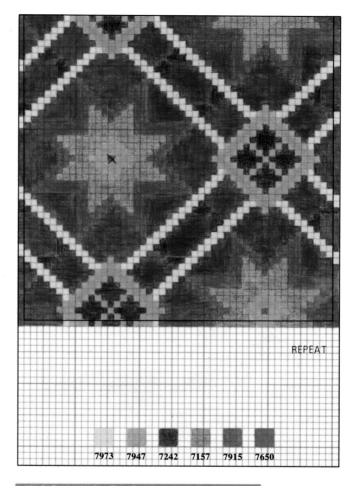

REPEAT

7973 7947 7242 7157 7915 7650

WORKING THE EMBROIDERY

1 Begin stitching at the centre of the design and work the main part (all the areas not colored blue on the chart) of the design in leviathan stitch (page 167). Each leviathan stitch is represented by a colored square on the chart and is worked over two vertical and two horizontal double threads of canvas.

2 When the leviathan stitch areas have been completed, stitch the blue areas in diagonal satin stitch (page 166) worked over two double canvas threads.

FINISHING THE CUSHION COVER

1 Press the embroidery lightly on the wrong side while it is still mounted on the stretcher. Use a warm iron and take care not to press too hard and crush the stitching. If the canvas has become distorted during the stitching, remove it from the stretcher and block it (page 172).

2 Cut away the surplus canvas round the edge of the embroidery, leaving a margin of about ½ in (1.5 cm) along each side for the seam allowance. Cut out two pieces of furnishing fabric for the back. Follow the instructions on page 157 for making up the cover.

THE BLUE AREAS on the chart represent diagonal satin stitch. This is a flat stitch which *contrasts well with the textured surface produced by the leviathan stitch design.*

MIDDLE EASTERN PATTERN LIBRARY

CHAPTER NINE

SOUTH AND SOUTH-EAST ASIA

South Asia, a wedge-shaped area of land jutting into the Indian Ocean, is the most densely populated region on earth. This area contains India and Pakistan, lands of tremendous geographical and economic contrasts which have a rich and ancient tradition of native arts and crafts. South-East Asia, a term originally coined in the 1900s to describe a trading area to the south of China, stretches eastwards from the borders of India and includes Thailand, Singapore, Indonesia and Malaysia inside its boundaries. The complex mix of peoples, religions, climatic conditions and natural features in South-East Asia is reflected in the wide range of traditional crafts varying from the appliquéd and embroidered full-pleated skirts of Thailand's Blue Hmong tribe to the exquisitely carved and painted shadow puppets of Indonesia.

Shisha embroidery is an ancient Indian textile technique worked by attaching discs of mirror or tin to a piece of fabric by making an embroidered surround to hold them in place. The discs are called shisha glass or shisha mirrors (the word 'shisha' actually means 'little glass') and they are made in various colors – silver, which is the traditional color, as well as gold, green and blue. Traditional shisha glass is hand-cut and the discs have irregular edges which are covered by the embroidered surround. The origins of shisha embroidery are many centuries old – Mumtaz-i-Mahal, the wife of the Moghul emperor of India, Shah Jahan (1592–1666), is believed to have developed the technique in the early years of the 17th century. After her death, Shah Jahan commemorated his wife by building a beautiful white marble mausoleum, the Taj Mahal, in Agra, northern India.

Shisha embroidery is still worked today, notably in the states of Gujarat and Punjab in India, the province of Sind in Pakistan and also in Afghanistan, and modern methods are practically identical to the old techniques. Indian embroiderers apply shisha glass to skirts and bodices, bags, ceremonial trappings for animals, and torans, richly embroidered friezes which hang over doorways or windows on festive occasions. The shoulder bag on page 140 recreates a piece of early 19th-century shisha embroidery from Gujarat. The traditional design has been brought up to date and adapted for cross stitch, with the pieces of shisha glass replaced by circular groups of tiny silver beads.

Hundreds of species of epiphytic and terrestrial orchids grow wild throughout the moist tropical regions of South-East Asia. Orchid flowers are exotic to look at and can vary dramatically in size, shape and color from species to species. The most common wild orchids in this area include Dendrobium, Phalaenopsis (moth orchids), Paphiopedilum (slipper orchids) and Cymbidium, all of which have been hybridized by botanists during recent years to achieve larger, more colorful blooms with the long-lasting properties which are essential for the commercial market. Singapore is world-famous for its orchids, many of which are produced by growers specially for the florist trade and are flown regularly across the world to delight us with their spectacular blooms. The ornate silver-plated dressing table set on page 142 is decorated with a delicate orchid and trellis pattern worked in shades of pink, mauve and green. A selection of charted orchid designs is given in the pattern library on page 145, including large flowerheads, small single motifs and a deep repeating border. You may like to use commercially shaded stranded cotton when stitching the designs, or prefer to make up your own mixtures by combining two or more strands of toning colors of thread in your needle at the same time. The palm tree motif decorating the tablecloth on page 146 is a reminder of the unspoilt and unpolluted scenery still to be found in some parts of South and South-East Asia, particularly on the small islands set in the warm, blue waters of the Indian Ocean. Although some of the islands in the larger, more well-known groups such as the Seychelles are developing rapidly to meet the increasing demands of tourism, island groups like the Maldives and the Comores remain relatively untouched – a true tropical paradise. The corner motif shows palm trees surrounded by lush vegetation, golden sands and sparkling blue water and it makes the perfect decoration for a picnic cloth.

The tribal peoples living in the hills which straddle the borders of south-west China, Laos, Thailand and Burma have a long tradition of embroidery, decorating both their everyday clothes and special costumes for festive occasions. The embroidered

designs vary from region to region, and they also change with the age and status of the wearer and the type of occasion on which an individual garment will be worn. Their fabrics are often dyed indigo or black, then embroidered with geometric patterns in bright thread colors. The patterns are usually worked in cross stitch and are composed of solid diamonds, zigzags, eight-pointed stars, interlaced and serrated lines, swastikas and spirals. The embroidered garment is decorated with many three-dimensional objects including silver beads and discs, thread tassels and pompoms, cowrie shells, buttons and large colored seeds.

The purse on page 148 is decorated with a typical Thai design worked in bright colors, but here a pale green fabric has been used instead of the traditional indigo or black background. The purse is made from one piece of fabric which is first embroidered, then lined with silk to cover the raw edges. Next, three corners are folded over and the adjacent edges oversewn to form a pocket, with the fourth corner serving as the flap. The purse can easily be made into a bag by stitching four repeats of the design, and you may like to decorate it with tassels and pompoms.

Investigate the following sources for more South and South-East Asian designs: the delicate carved marble patterns inlaid with precious stones on the Taj Mahal; Moghul miniatures and Rajput palace decorations; paisley shawl designs and floral papier mâché boxes from Kashmir; embroidery designs for curtained elephant howdahs, sari fabrics, marriage canopies; golden Buddhas and the multi-colored mosaic mirror work of Thai temples; exotic batik sarong prints from Malaysia and Indonesia; Punjabi phulkari cloths decorated with darned patterns; Chikan whitework embroidery from Lucknow; the bas reliefs on the elaborately carved Hindu temples of Angkor Wat and Angkor Thom in Cambodia.

THE COMPLEX mix of peoples, religions and cultures in this region is reflected in a broad array of traditional arts and crafts, ranging from stone carving to intricate metalwork.

GUJARATI
SHOULDER BAG

The north-western state of Gujarat produces some of the most colorful embroideries stitched in India, including those decorated with shisha embroidery which is also known as mirror work. This design has been adapted from a piece of traditional shisha embroidery, but here the pieces of mirror glass have been replaced by silver beads.

MATERIALS

- Red 11 count Pearl Aida evenweave fabric 43 in (110 cm) wide (Zweigart E1007, color 954 Christmas red)
- Matching silk or cotton fabric for lining
- Red grosgrain ribbon about ½ in (6 m'm) wide
- 25 round, flat silver beads or sequins
- 444 small round silver beads
- 8 fish-shaped silver beads (or any other long shape)
- DMC stranded cotton in the following colors: purple 333; red 321; orange 971; yellow 307; green 702; dark grey 3799
- Tapestry needle size 24
- Crewel needles sizes 6 and 8
- Tacking thread in a light color
- Sewing needle and pins
- Matching sewing thread
- Adjustable rectangular embroidery frame

MEASURING UP

The finished bag measures 7½ in (19 cm) wide and 8½ in (21.5 cm) deep, and it is made from a strip of fabric which is folded roughly in three to make a pocket covered by a square flap. About 1 in (2.5 cm) of the pocket should appear below the flap. You will need one piece of evenweave fabric approximately 9 in (23 cm) wide and three times the depth of the bag, plus a piece of lining fabric the same size. You will need to add at least 4 in (10 cm) all round to these measurements to allow you to mount the fabric in the frame.

PREPARING THE FABRIC

Mark out the outline of the bag on the evenweave fabric with rows of tacking. Then, mark the finished size of the embroidered area at one end of the fabric, placing the edge of the embroidery 3 fabric blocks inside the tacked outline. Use rows of tacking and make the area

79 blocks square. Tack vertical and horizontal lines through the tacked square to mark the centre of the embroidery.

WORKING THE EMBROIDERY

1 Mark the centre of the chart with a soft pencil. Mount the fabric in the embroidery frame (page 160).
2 Work the design in cross stitch (page 164) from the chart, using three strands of thread in the tapestry needle. Begin at the centre of the design and work outwards, remembering that each square on the chart represents one cross stitch worked over one vertical and one horizontal fabric block.
3 Use half cross stitch (page 165) to attach 37 small silver beads inside each circle of dark grey cross stitch, attaching one bead with every stitch you make. Work with two strands of red thread in the size 8 crewel needle. Then, use a group of four straight stitches radiating from the same hole to attach a single flat bead to the centre of each of the unworked squares. Use six strands of red thread in the size 6 crewel needle.

MAKING UP THE BAG

1 Before removing the embroidery from the frame, press it gently on the wrong side with a warm iron. Remove it from the frame. Cut away the surplus fabric from round the edge, leaving about ½ in (1.5 cm) for turnings all round.
2 Turn under the raw edges along the tacked outline and tack them in place. Turn under the raw edges of the lining in the same way, making the lining slightly smaller than the main fabric. Place the fabric and the lining with wrong sides facing and tack both pieces together round the edges. Machine stitch along the short edge furthest from the embroidery.
3 Fold this end up by about one-third so that you form a pocket about 8¼ in (21 cm) deep. Pin and tack the pocket in place. Fold the embroidered end over the pocket to make a flap. The flap should allow about 1 in (2.5 cm) of the pocket to show along the bottom of the bag.
4 Unfold the flap and machine stitch close to the edge along the two long edges and across the bottom of the flap. Stitch 8 silver fish along the bottom of the flap, positioning them in groups of 2. Use six strands of red thread in the size 6 crewel needle and finish the thread ends off neatly.
5 Stitch the ends of the ribbon securely underneath the flap to make a strap. Fold the flap over the pocket.

THE CHART SHOWS all the embroidered areas, and one square on the chart represents one complete stitch worked over one fabric block. The round and flat beads are stitched on to the fabric after the cross stitch pattern has been completed, and the fish-shaped beads added after the bag has been made up.

MAKE THIS beaded bag to hold your purse, make-up and keys for a special night out. Here, the colors of the threads and beads have been chosen to complement the red fabric, but you could choose a different color scheme to match your outfit, perhaps substituting gold beads for silver.

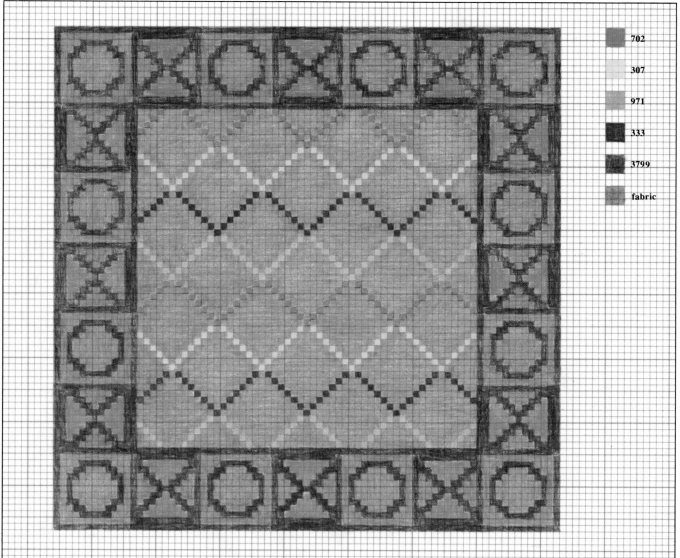

	702
	307
	971
	333
	3799
	fabric

SINGAPORE
ORCHIDS DRESSING TABLE SET

Singapore is world famous for its beautiful orchids which are airfreighted to destinations on almost every continent. This intricately worked silver-plated dressing table set, decorated with an orchid and trellis stitched in pink, mauve and green, would make a very special gift.

MATERIALS

- Antique white 11 count Pearl Aida evenweave fabric 43 in (110 cm) wide (Zweigart E1007, color 101)
- Medium weight iron-on interfacing
- Silver-plated dressing table set (available from Framecraft, see page 4)
- DMC stranded cotton in the following colors: pinks 603, 718; mauve 208; green 3348
- Tapestry needle size 24
- Tacking thread in a dark color
- Sewing needle
- Large embroidery hoop

MEASURING UP

You will need two pieces of fabric, each one about 4 in (10 cm) larger all round than the mirror and the hairbrush backs to allow you to mount the fabric in the hoop during stitching.

PREPARING THE FABRIC

Following the manufacturer's instructions, carefully take the mirror and the hairbrush to pieces. Lay the two acetate pieces on your fabric and carefully tack round the edge of each piece. These lines denote the finished size of each embroidery. Next tack a vertical line through the centre of the fabric inside each tacked outline, taking care not to cross any vertical threads. Mark the central horizontal lines in the same way and mark the centre of both charts with a soft pencil. Mount the fabric in the embroidery hoop (page 160).

THIS ELEGANT dressing table set is silver-plated and specially designed to display pieces of fine embroidery. A matching clothes brush is also available, or you could choose a plainer, gold-colored version of the set.

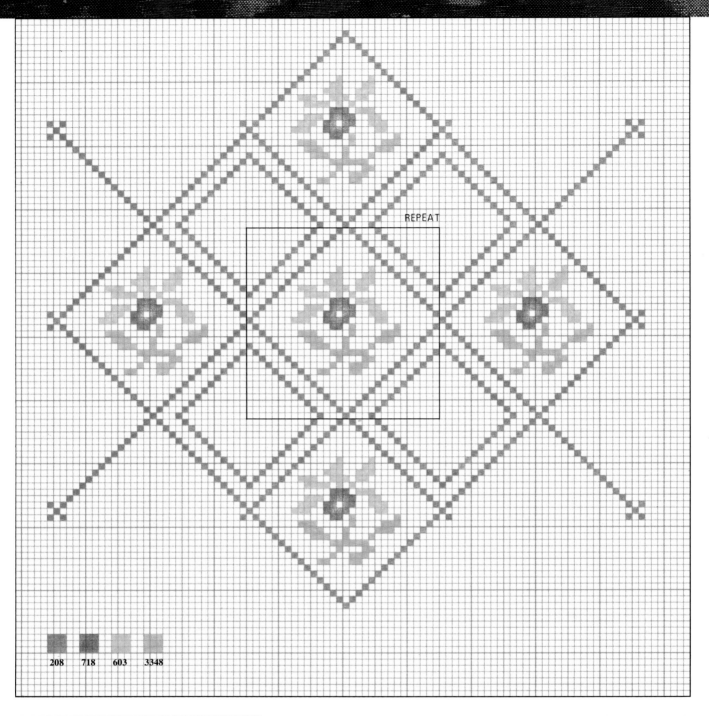

REPEAT

| 208 | 718 | 603 | 3348 |

WORKING THE EMBROIDERY

Both designs are worked in the same way.

1 Begin working the design in cross stitch (page 164) at the centre of the fabric. Use three strands of thread in the needle throughout and note that each colored square on the chart represents one cross stitch worked over one vertical and one horizontal woven block of fabric. Continue the embroidery right up to the tacked outline to avoid unsightly gaps in the stitching when the mirror and the hairbrush are reassembled.

MAKING UP THE SET

1 When all the embroidery has been completed, press it lightly on the wrong side over a well-padded surface.

WORK THE all-over orchid and trellis design from the chart to fill both the mirror and the hairbrush backs. Make sure you *take the stitching right up to the edge of the tacked shape so that no unsightly gaps occur in the pattern.*

Use a warm iron and take care not to press too hard and crush the stitching.

2 Iron a piece of interfacing on to the reverse of each piece of embroidery and allow to cool. Cut out the fabric along the tacked lines.

3 Reassemble the mirror and the hairbrush with the embroideries in position, taking care to follow the manufacturer's instructions.

ORCHIDS PATTERN LIBRARY

PALM TREES
TABLECLOTH

A tablecloth decorated with tiny palm trees conjures up the sparkling blue seas and golden sandy beaches of the unspoilt tropical islands of South-East Asia. The cloth is the perfect partner for an al fresco meal of exotic tropical delicacies.

MATERIALS

- Antique white 18 count Ainring evenweave fabric 51 in (130 cm) wide (Zweigart E3793, color 101)
- DMC stranded cotton in the following colors: gold 977; kingfisher 996; turquoise 959; greens 580, 906, 907, 911; browns 610, 632
- Tapestry needle size 24
- Crewel needle size 8
- Tacking thread in a dark color
- Sewing needle and pins
- Embroidery hoop

MEASURING UP

The palm trees design can be used to decorate any size of square or rectangular tablecloth, but remember that the width of the fabric you choose will limit the size of the finished cloth. To make a cloth to fit a particular table, first measure the length and width of the table top. Decide how far the cloth will hang down over the edge of the table and add twice this measurement to each of the table top measurements. Finally, add 2 in (5 cm) all round for the hem allowance.

PREPARING THE FABRIC

Tack a guideline round the cloth 4 in (10 cm) in from the position of the finished edge. On the chart, the design covers an area 48 squares wide and 45 squares deep, with each colored square representing one stitch worked over two vertical and two horizontal woven blocks of fabric. At each corner of the guideline, mark out a rectangle 96 blocks wide by 90 blocks deep with lines of tacking to accommodate the palm trees motif.

WORKING THE EMBROIDERY

1 Tack a vertical line through the centre of each rectangle, taking care not to cross any vertical threads, then tack along the central horizontal line in the same way. Mark the centre of the chart with a soft pencil.
2 Mount the fabric in the embroidery hoop (page 160), and work the design in cross stitch (page 164) from the chart, using three strands of thread in the tapestry needle. Start stitching at the centre and work outwards, remembering that each square on the chart represents one cross stitch worked over two vertical and two horizontal fabric blocks.

MAKING UP THE TABLECLOTH

1 Press the embroidery lightly on the wrong side with a warm iron over a well-padded surface.
2 Fold over ¾ in (2 cm) round the raw edge, then a further 1¼ in (3 cm) to make an uneven hem (page 169) round the cloth and mitre the corners (page 171). Make sure that the hemline fold runs neatly between two rows of fabric blocks.
3 Work a row of back stitch (page 164) round the tablecloth, positioning it just below the turned-over edge of the hem. Use two strands of turquoise thread in the crewel needle and work the stitches over two fabric blocks.

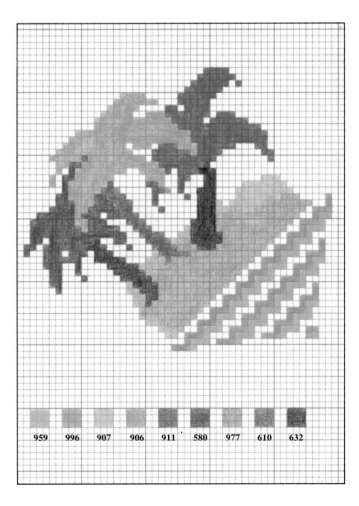

| 959 | 996 | 907 | 906 | 911 | 580 | 977 | 610 | 632 |

EACH COLORED *square represents one complete cross stitch worked over two vertical and two horizontal fabric blocks. Work the palm tree design in shades of green, brown and blue, using three strands of thread.*

EMBROIDER THE *tropical island motifs and make a fun cloth for a picnic meal on a hot summer's day. You could isolate a single palm tree from the chart and use this to decorate a set of napkins, following the making up instructions given on page 82.*

THAI
PURSE

The women of the hill tribes of Thailand use cross stitch to decorate their colorful garments, often combining it with satin stitch and appliquéd fabric. This tiny coin purse features a typically symmetrical Thai design worked in bright colors. To make a larger purse or bag, simply work four complete repeats of the design instead of just one.

MATERIALS

- Small piece of pale green 11 count Pearl Aida even-weave fabric 43 in (110 cm) wide (Zweigart E1007, color 617 mint)
- Small piece of silk lining fabric
- Tiny pearl button
- DMC stranded cotton in the following colors: purple 333; red 816; yellow 307; kingfisher 996; blue 798; pale green 504
- Tapestry needle size 24
- Crewel needle size 7
- Tacking thread in a dark color
- Sewing needle and pins
- Large embroidery hoop

MEASURING UP

The finished embroidery measures 4¼ in (11 cm) square. You will need to add ½ in (1.5 cm) all round for turnings, plus about 4 in (10 cm) all round to allow you to mount the fabric in the embroidery hoop while you are stitching. You will also need a piece of lining fabric 4¼ in (11 cm) square plus turnings.

PREPARING THE FABRIC

Tack a vertical line through the centre of the evenweave fabric, taking care not to cross any vertical threads. Mark the central horizontal line in the same way. Mount the fabric in the embroidery hoop or frame (page 160) and mark the centre of the chart with a soft pencil.

WORKING THE EMBROIDERY

Begin working the design in cross stitch (page 164) at the centre of the fabric. Use three strands of thread in the tapestry needle and note that each colored square on the chart represents one stitch worked over one vertical and one horizontal woven block of fabric.

MAKING UP THE PURSE

1 When all the embroidery has been completed, press it lightly on the wrong side over a well-padded surface. Use a warm iron and take care not to press too hard and crush the stitching.

2 Cut away the surplus fabric round the embroidery, leaving a margin of about ¾ in (2 cm) all round. Turn under the raw edges, leaving a strip of two fabric blocks showing all round the embroidery. Turn under the raw edges of the lining and place on top of the embroidery with wrong sides facing. Slipstitch (page 168) the lining to the embroidered fabric.

3 Place the embroidery face down on a flat surface. Turn three of the corners over on to the right side to form a pocket like an envelope, making sure that the three corners meet neatly. Oversew (page 168) the sides together, using three strands of pale green thread in the crewel needle and taking each stitch through pairs of opposite holes in the fabric.

4 Make a buttonhole loop (page 171) on the remaining corner and sew on the button at the point where the other three corners meet. Fold over the fourth corner to close the purse.

5 When making a larger bag, work more complete repeats of the pattern and add a length of heavy braid or ribbon to make a shoulder strap.

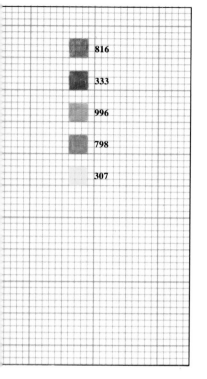

	816
	333
	996
	798
	307

TO MAKE A *larger purse or a bag, simply repeat the chart pattern four times to make a bigger square of embroidery, then finish it off in the same way as for the small purse. Each colored square represents one cross stitch worked over one woven fabric block.*

EASILY CONSTRUCTED *by folding and oversewing a square of embroidered fabric, this tiny coin purse is decorated with a geometric design made up of brightly colored elements.*

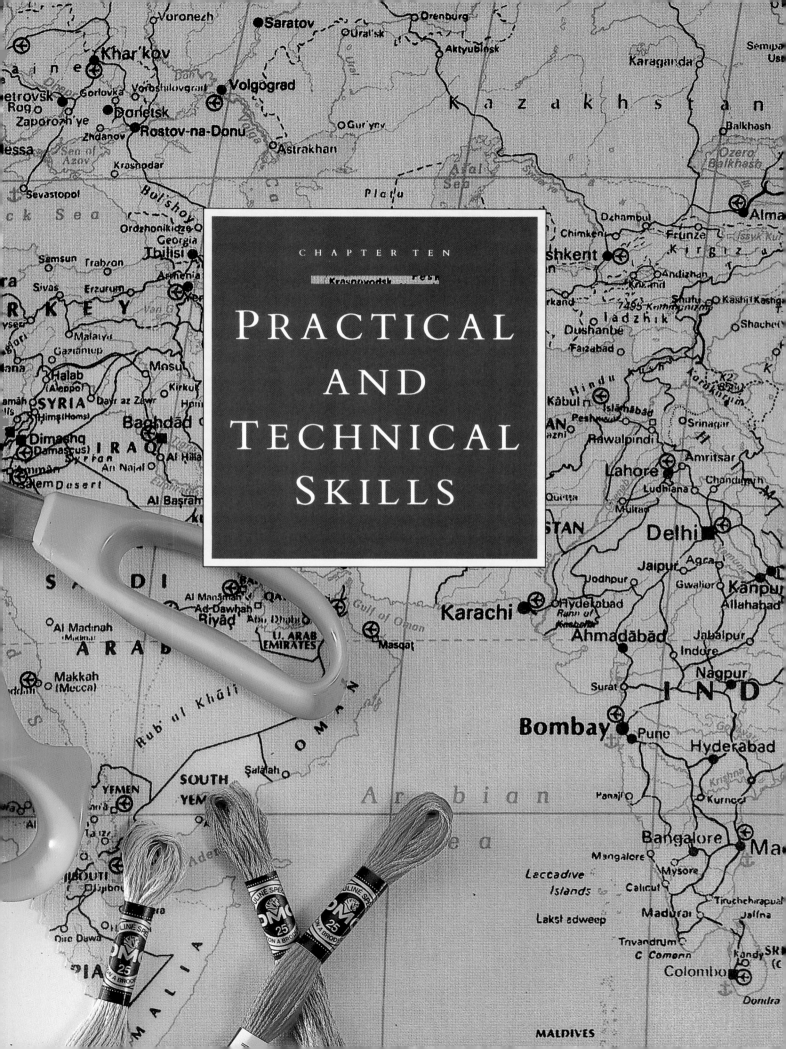

CHAPTER TEN

PRACTICAL
AND
TECHNICAL
SKILLS

MAKING UP THE PROJECTS

PATTERNS

To enlarge the pattern pieces to the correct size, copy the shapes square-by-square on to dressmaker's pattern paper, remembering that each square on the grid shown here represents one 2 in (5 cm) square on the pattern paper. After drawing the outlines on to your paper, mark each piece with the appropriate name and take care to transfer any other information such as dots, notches or pocket positions.

Each pattern piece already includes the appropriate seam allowances ½ in (1.5 cm) and hem allowances, but you must always remember to add on at least 4 in (10 cm) all round when the pieces are to be embroidered. This margin is to allow you to mount the fabric comfortably and securely in a hoop or frame while you are working the embroidery.

MAKING UP THE WAISTCOAT

1 Turn a narrow double hem along the top of the pocket and hem (page 168) neatly by hand. Turn under the other three sides of the pocket and pin it on to the right front as indicated on the pattern. Machine stitch round three sides.

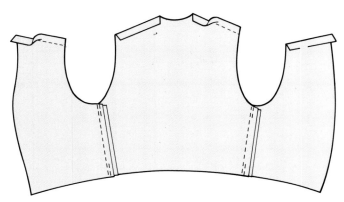

2 Pin and stitch the waistcoat back to each waistcoat front at the sides. Repeat with the lining pieces. Stitch ½ in (1.5 cm) away from the raw edge along the shoulder edges of the lining and press under along the line of stitching.

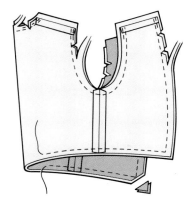

3 Pin the lining and the waistcoat together with right sides facing, and stitch the armhole, neck, front and lower edges, leaving an opening along the lower edge for turning.

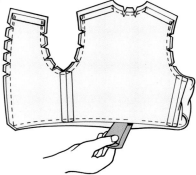

4 Turn the waistcoat right side out through the opening, then slipstitch (page 168) the opening closed. Stitch across the shoulder seams, leaving the lining free. Press the shoulder seams open with your fingers and slipstitch (page 168) the shoulder edges of the lining together. Machine topstitch (page 168) round the edges with matching thread, then press the waistcoat lightly on the right side.

ELIZABETHAN HERB BAG

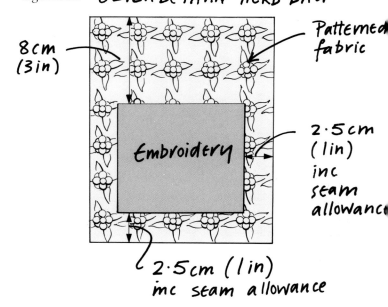

8cm (3in)

Patterned fabric

Embroidery

2·5cm (1in) inc seam allowance

2·5cm (1in) inc seam allowance

MAKING UP THE CHRISTENING GOWN

1 Pin the yoke front lining and the embroidered yoke front together with wrong sides facing and treat this as a single piece of fabric. Stitch the front yoke to the back yoke along the shoulder seams.

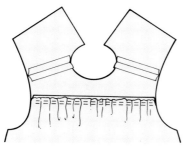

2 Gather (page 171) the upper edge of the front, pin and stitch it to the lower edge of the yoke front. Press the seam towards the yoke. Repeat for the back. Stitch the centre back seam to the dot and press the seam open. Turn a narrow double hem (page 169) along the centre back opening and hand hem (page 168) it in place.

3 Stitch the side seams and press open. Gather (page 171) the sleeve tops between the notches. Stitch the underarm seam and turn up the lower edge to form a casing for the elastic. Stitch round the casing close to the inner edge and leave an opening for the elastic.

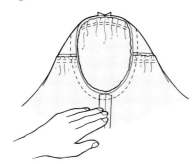

4 With right sides together and matching sleeve dot with shoulder seam, pin the sleeve into the armhole, pulling up the gathers to fit and matching the underarm seams. Stitch round the armhole and clip the curves.

5 Bind (page 170) the neck edge with satin binding, leaving about 12 in (30 cm) of binding free at each end to make ties. Slipstitch (page 168) along the ties. Bind the lower edge of the gown with satin binding. Insert elastic in the sleeve casings, adjust to fit, sew ends together securely and stitch the opening closed.

MAKING UP THE DUFFLE BAG

1 Fold the body piece in half with right sides together and stitch the centre back seam. Press the seam open. Repeat with the body lining. Place the lining inside the body with wrong sides facing and lower edges matching and tack round the upper and lower edges of the lining. Place the base pieces together with wrong sides facing and tack round the edge.

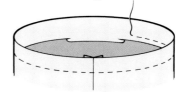

2 Turn the upper edge of the bag over along the foldline, turning under ¼ in (6 mm) along the raw edge. Press and pin in place. Machine stitch close to the inner edge. Pin the base to the lower edge of the body, matching seam to dot. Stitch twice round the base to make a strong seam.

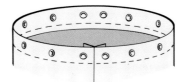

3 Following the manufacturer's instructions, apply an eyelet to each position marked on the pattern. Thread ribbon or cord through the eyelets and adjust to fit. Join the ends securely and gather up the bag.

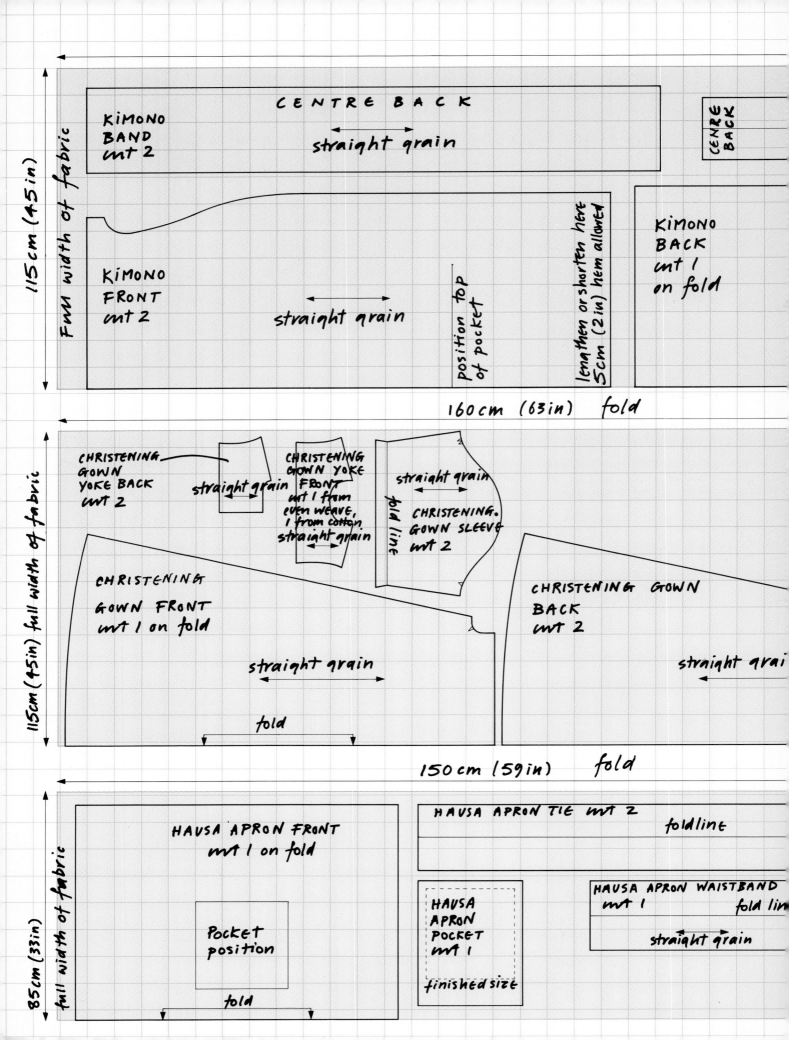

Top layout (115cm / 45in full width of fabric, 160cm / 63in fold):

KIMONO BAND cut 2

CENTRE BACK

straight grain

CENTRE BACK

KIMONO FRONT cut 2

straight grain

position top of pocket

lengthen or shorten here 5cm (2in) hem allowed

KIMONO BACK cut 1 on fold

Full width of fabric 115cm (45in)

160cm (63in) fold

Middle layout (115cm / 45in full width of fabric, 150cm / 59in fold):

CHRISTENING GOWN YOKE BACK cut 2

straight grain

CHRISTENING GOWN YOKE FRONT cut 1 from even weave, 1 from cotton straight grain

straight grain

fold line

CHRISTENING GOWN SLEEVE cut 2

CHRISTENING GOWN FRONT cut 1 on fold

straight grain

fold

CHRISTENING GOWN BACK cut 2

straight grain

115cm (45in) full width of fabric

150cm (59in) fold

Bottom layout (85cm / 33in full width of fabric):

HAUSA APRON FRONT cut 1 on fold

Pocket position

fold

HAUSA APRON TIE cut 2

foldline

HAUSA APRON POCKET cut 1

finished size

HAUSA APRON WAISTBAND cut 1

fold line

straight grain

85cm (33in) full width of fabric

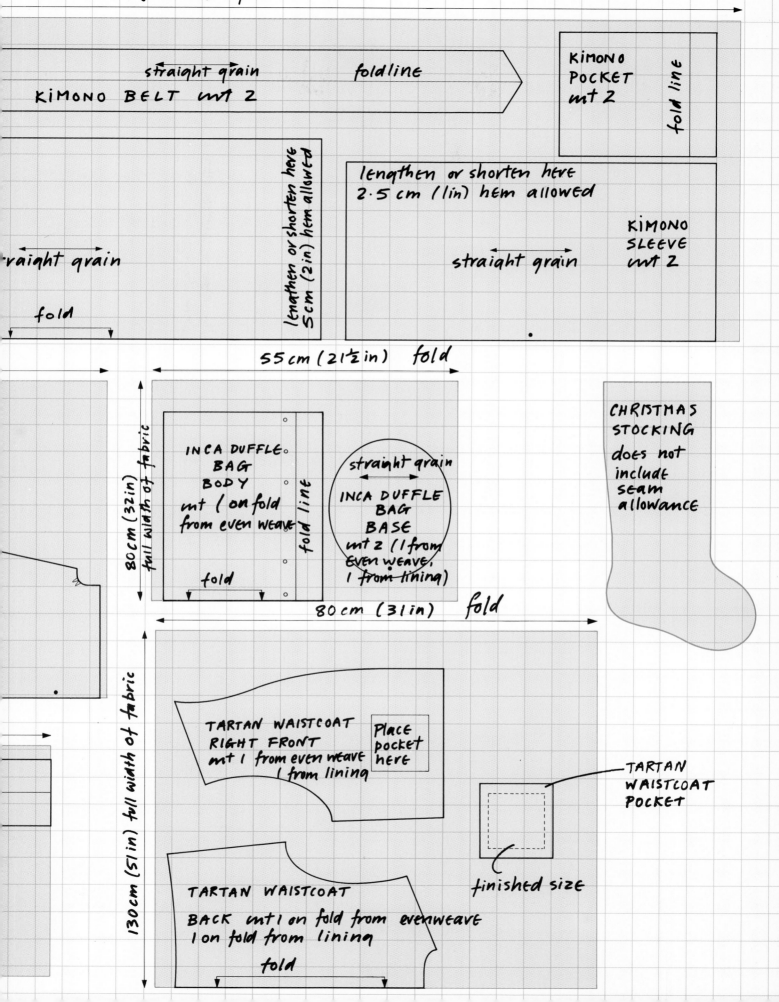

270 cm (106 in) fold

straight grain   foldline

KIMONO BELT cut 2

KIMONO POCKET cut 2

fold line

lengthen or shorten here 5cm (2in) hem allowed

lengthen or shorten here 2·5 cm (1in) hem allowed

straight grain

fold

straight grain

KIMONO SLEEVE cut 2

55 cm (21½ in) fold

80 cm (32in) full width of fabric

INCA DUFFLE BAG BODY cut 1 on fold from even weave

fold line

fold

straight grain

INCA DUFFLE BAG BASE cut 2 (1 from even weave, 1 from lining)

CHRISTMAS STOCKING does not include seam allowance

80 cm (31 in) fold

130cm (51in) full width of fabric

TARTAN WAISTCOAT RIGHT FRONT cut 1 from even weave 1 from lining

Place pocket here

TARTAN WAISTCOAT POCKET

finished size

TARTAN WAISTCOAT BACK cut 1 on fold from evenweave 1 on fold from lining

fold

MAKING UP THE KIMONO

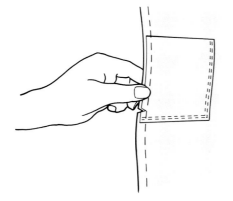

1 Turn an uneven hem (page 169) along the top of the pockets and machine stitch close to the inner edge. Pin the pockets in position on the kimono fronts, as indicated on the pattern, tack along the seamline and stitch the pockets in place on the fronts with two rows of machine stitching.

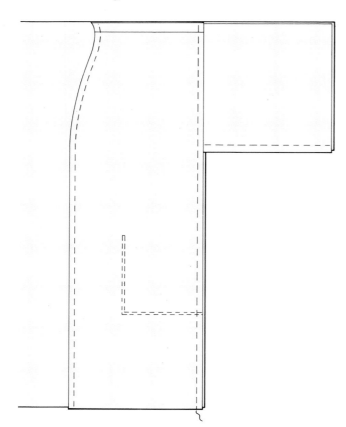

2 Pin the shoulder seams and stitch. Matching sleeve dot to shoulder seam, pin the sleeve to the armhole edge and stitch. Folding the seam away from the sleeve, pin and stitch the sleeve seam, keeping the body seam allowance free.

3 Press the seam allowance towards the sleeve. Stitch the side seam to the hem, keeping the sleeve seam allowance free. Press the seam towards the back. Turn an uneven hem (page 169) along the lower edge of the sleeves and machine stitch.

4 Join the band pieces with a plain seam (page 168) at the centre back. Fold in half lengthways and press, then turn under ½ in (1.5 cm) along the two long edges and press in place. Apply the band along the front and neck edges in the same way as applying bias binding (page 170), matching the centre back band seam to the centre of the neck edge. Press the band.

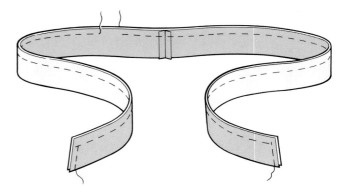

5 Turn up the hem allowance into an uneven hem (page 169) and machine stitch. Join the belt pieces at the centre back, fold along the foldline and stitch round three sides, leaving an opening close to the centre back seam. Turn to the right side, press and slipstitch (page 168) the opening closed. Make the carriers for the belt by working a buttonhole loop (page 171) at each side of the kimono with matching thread. Give the kimono a final light press.

LOG CABIN CUSHION

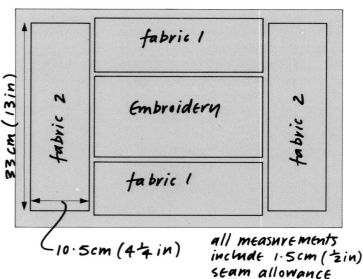

fabric 1

fabric 2

Embroidery

fabric 2

fabric 1

33 cm (13 in)

10.5 cm (4¼ in)

all measurements include 1.5 cm (½ in) seam allowance

MAKING UP THE CUSHION COVER

The simplest way to make a plain cushion cover is to stitch the front and back pieces together round the edge, leaving an opening along one side. Slipstitch (page 168) the opening closed after the cushion pad has been added. On a larger cushion, it looks neater to close the opening with a zip fastener.

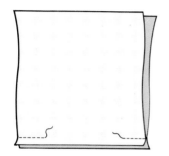

1 Pin the front and back pieces together and stitch about 2 in (5 cm) at either end of the opening. Press the seams flat.

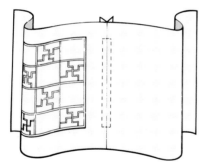

2 Pin, tack and machine stitch the zip fastener along the opening.

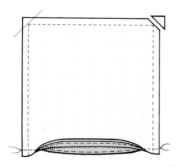

3 Open the zip fastener and stitch round the remaining three sides of the cushion. Clip the corners (page 169) to reduce bulk, then turn to the right side and press.

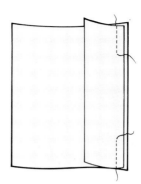

4 When the cushion front has been embroidered right to the edge, insert the zip fastener in a seam across the cushion back for a really neat finish. Position the seam either centrally or at one side of the fabric, stitching about 2 in (5 cm) at each end.

5 Follow step 2, above. Then open the zip fastener, place front and back together with right sides facing and stitch round all four sides. Clip the corners (page 169), then turn the cover to the right side and press.

MAKING UP THE NOTEBOOK COVER

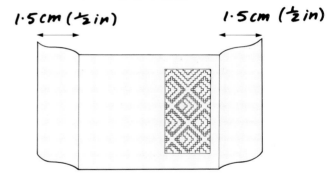

1.5 CM (½ in)   1.5 CM (½ in)

1 Turn a narrow double hem at each end of the cover and machine stitch. Neaten the raw edges along the top and bottom of the cover with a row of blanket stitch (page 166) or by working machine zigzag. Turn ½ in (1.5 cm) to the wrong side along these edges and tack in place.

2 Lay the cover on a flat surface, right side downwards, and lay the notebook on top. Fold over about 2 in (5 cm) of the cover at each side of the notebook to form flaps and pin in place.

3 Remove the notebook. Secure the flaps by working a row of back stitch (page 164) right round the cover using two strands of cream thread in the size 7 crewel needle. Position the back stitches two fabric blocks from the edge of the cover and work each stitch over two fabric blocks. Slide the notebook under the flaps.

157

EMBROIDERY TECHNIQUES

Cross stitch embroidery is easy to work, even for the inexperienced stitcher, and you will quickly become confident enough to work complicated designs in many colors of thread. For all but the smallest designs, stretch your fabric in a hoop or frame as this will help you stitch evenly and accurately.

Exact quantities of materials are not given for each project. Instead, there are details of how to measure up and calculate your own fabric requirements for each item. Estimate the amount of thread required by using one complete skein of each color and measuring how much of the design has been completed. Many of the small projects need less than one skein of each color, and are the ideal way to use up any oddments you may have lying around.

If you are left-handed, many of the diagrams will be easier to follow if you prop the book up in front of a mirror and then follow the reflected images.

CHOOSING FABRIC AND CANVAS

An evenweave fabric is the best choice for cross stitch embroidery as it has the same number of identical threads to every 1 in (2.5 cm) of fabric. The weight varies from fine to coarse, with fine fabrics having more threads or blocks to each 1 in (2.5 cm) than the coarse ones have. The number of threads is called the count, or gauge, and these threads are counted so that stitches can be worked accurately from a chart. The most popular type of evenweave fabric for cross stitch embroidery is made from cotton and has groups of threads woven together to produce distinct blocks over which the stitches are worked. These fabrics, called Aida, Ainring, Hardanger and Binca, are available in different counts and in a good color range which includes pastels and bright colors. Other fabrics suitable for cross stitch include evenweaves made from linen, linen/cotton mixtures and cotton/synthetic mixtures.

Canvas is constructed in a similar way to evenweave fabric, but it produces a regular grid or mesh of stiffened threads which are usually covered by the stitching. In single canvas (also known as petit point or mono canvas) the grid is produced by single warp and weft threads, while the grid of double canvas (also known as Penelope canvas) is made up of pairs of warp and weft threads. Canvas is available in a wide range of mesh sizes and the number of threads is quoted per 1 in (2.5 cm) in a similar way to the count of evenweave fabric. For example, 17 mesh canvas means that there are 17 threads to every 1 in (2.5 cm) of canvas.

CHOOSING THREADS AND NEEDLES

Many of the projects in this book have been stitched with stranded cotton. This is the most versatile embroidery thread available, as each length is constructed from six loosely twisted strands and can be split up into different weights to suit the fabric weight and the size of the intended stitches. Always separate all six strands and then recombine the appropriate number you are using in the needle. Strands of several colors can be used together in the needle to make your own multi-colored thread for shading. Stranded cotton has a slight sheen and comes in an extensive color range.

Cotton perlé, also called pearl cotton, is a shiny, twisted thread which cannot be divided into separate strands. This thread is made in three different weights (3, 5 and 8) but No. 5 is the most readily available and it has a good range of colors. One length of cotton perlé No. 5 is slightly heavier in weight than six strands of stranded cotton.

Tapestry wool is a thick, slightly twisted pure wool thread which cannot be divided into strands and is available in a wide color range. The thread is both colorfast and treated to be resistant to moth damage and, when it is stitched on canvas, it makes a heavy, hard-wearing surface suitable for covering cushions, chair seats and stool tops.

Use your threads in pieces no longer than 15 in (38 cm) to avoid tangling and fraying. Divide each skein of thread into convenient lengths by winding it round and round a piece of stiff card 15 in (38 cm) long, then cutting across the thread at each end. Make a loose plait from the cut lengths and remove each length as required by pulling one end gently from the plait.

Tapestry needles are used for embroidery on canvas, but they are also ideal for use with evenweave fabric as the blunt point separates the fabric threads easily without splitting them. They are available in sizes 14 to 26, graded from coarse (low numbers) to fine (high numbers). Crewel needles have long eyes and sharp points and should be used in preference to tapestry needles when working a decorative stitch through several layers of fabric to finish off a hem edge or when stitching a piece of evenweave fabric on to ordinary fabric.

THREADING THE NEEDLE

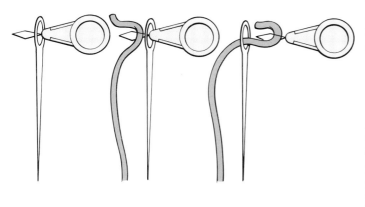

USING A NEEDLE THREADER

This is a small metal or plastic gadget with a wire loop at one end. Pass the loop through the needle eye, place the end of the thread in the loop and draw both loop and thread through the eye.

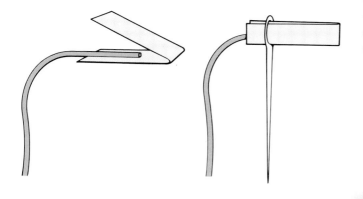

USING A PAPER STRIP

Cut a 2 in (5 cm) long strip of thin paper narrow enough to pass through the needle eye. Fold the strip in half to enclose the end of the thread. Thread the paper through the needle eye, pulling the thread through at the same time as the paper.

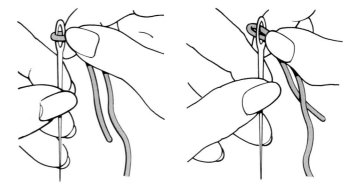

FOLDING THE THREAD

Fold the end of the thread round the needle top and pull it tight. Slip the folded thread off the needle and push it through the needle eye.

STARTING AND FINISHING

Never tie a knot at the end of the thread when working on either fabric or canvas. A knot can show through the finished piece of work and make an unsightly lump on the right side. A knot may also come undone during laundering, resulting in your stitching unravelling. Instead, secure the thread by making one or two tiny stitches in a space that will be covered by embroidery. Alternatively, leave about 2 in (5 cm) of thread hanging loose which can be darned in later.

When working an area which is partly stitched, secure the new thread neatly on the wrong side by sliding the needle under a group of stitches to anchor about 1 in (2.5 cm) of thread underneath them. To finish a length of thread, slide the needle under a group of stitches on the wrong side and cut off the loose end.

EMBROIDERY FRAMES

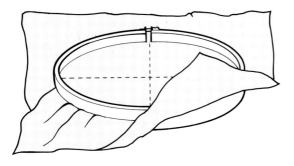
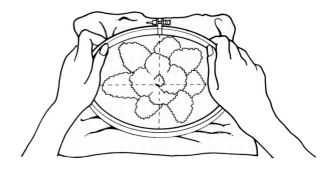

HOOPS

1 Embroidery hoops are available in various sizes and consist of two sections placed one inside the other. The fabric is sandwiched in between and the sections are secured by a screw at the side.

4 Loosen the screw and remove the larger hoop at the end of every stitching session. Press the fabric down with your thumbs at the edges of the hoop, lifting the larger hoop at the same time.

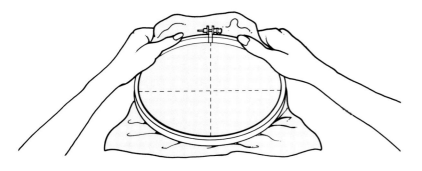
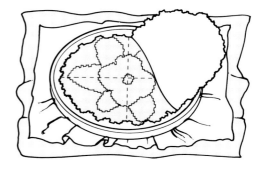

2 Spread the fabric, right side up, over the smaller hoop and press the larger hoop down over the top. Tighten the screw slightly until the larger hoop fits snugly round the smaller hoop.

5 Protect the area already worked by spreading a piece of tissue paper over the right side of the embroidery before it is remounted in the hoop. Cut away the paper to expose the next area to be worked.

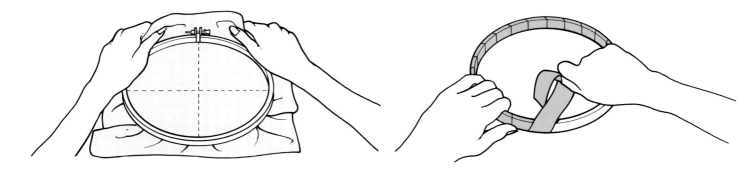

3 Manipulate the fabric with your fingers until it is evenly stretched, keeping the larger hoop pressed well down over the smaller hoop. Tighten the screw fully. Move the hoop along after one portion is completed.

6 Bind the smaller hoop, without the screw, with thin cotton tape to help prevent the fabric working loose and sagging as you stitch. The tape will also help avoid damage to delicate fabrics.

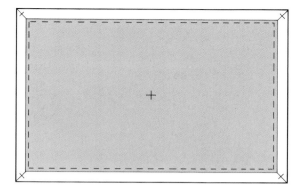

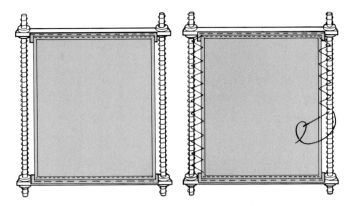

STRETCHER

This is a simple, non-adjustable frame made from four pieces of wood joined at the corners and it is used for stretching both fabric and canvas. Mark the centre of each side of the frame and the centre of each edge of the fabric. Working outwards from the centre of one side of the frame, line up the marks and attach the fabric or canvas to this side with drawing pins or staples. Repeat on the opposite side, making sure that the woven grain is straight, then attach the fabric or canvas to the other two sides of the stretcher in the same way.

3 Push the rods along the side arms so that the fabric is pulled taut, then move the nuts close to the rods and screw a locking nut on to each end of the side arms. Tighten all the nuts in turn so that the fabric is evenly stretched.

4 Lace the sides of the fabric to the sides of the frame with buttonhole thread, leaving a length of thread free at the top and bottom. Tighten the lacing from the centre outwards, working alternately along each side to tension the fabric evenly. Secure the thread ends by knotting them round the frame.

SLATE FRAME

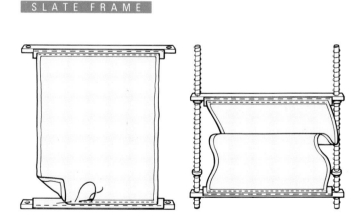

1 Turn over and tack ½ in (1.5 cm) all round the fabric. Mark the centre of the webbing on the rods, also mark the centre of the top and bottom of the fabric. Line up the marks and stitch the fabric to the webbing with back stitch (page 164), working from the centre point outwards. Use a strong thread such as buttonhole thread.

2 Screw two nuts on to each side arm and move them to the centre. Slot the top of the side arms into the holes in the top rod, then repeat at the bottom. When using a piece of fabric longer than the side arms, first roll the excess round one of the rods.

ROTATING FRAME

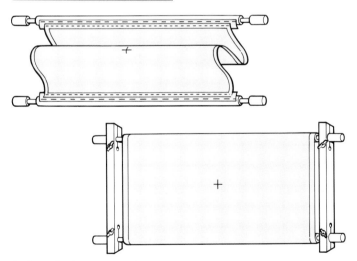

1 Attach the top and bottom of the fabric to the webbing on both the rollers by following the instructions given for a slate frame. Loosen the wing nuts on the side pieces and slot in the rollers, taking up any slack in the fabric by winding it round one of the rollers.

2 Turn the rollers to stretch the fabric and tighten the nuts firmly on the side pieces. Lace the fabric to the frame as for a slate frame. You may need to make several adjustments to get the tension even over the whole surface of the fabric.

WORKING FROM A CHART

Read the instructions given with each project carefully before you start to stitch. They will tell you how to mark the exact position of the embroidery on the fabric, and at which point on the chart you should start from. Usually this is the centre, and you will need to mark your starting point on the chart with a pencil mark which can be erased later. Beginning from the correct point and working outwards, embroider one stitch on the fabric for every coloured square shown on the chart. The instructions also tell you the number of woven fabric blocks you need to cover with each stitch so that the design will work out to the correct size.

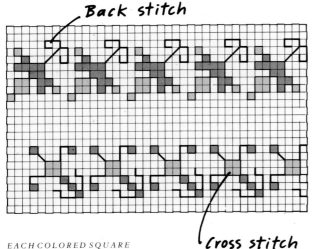

Back stitch

Cross stitch

EACH COLORED SQUARE
represents one stitch to be worked over one or more woven blocks of fabric. The instructions for each project – either in the main body of the text or the captions – specify the number of fabric blocks.

ADAPTING CROSS STITCH CHARTS

You can easily adapt ready-charted designs to suit your own purposes, whether they are those shown in the pattern libraries, charts for Fair Isle and picture knitting or needlepoint charts. You may, for example, want to make an all-over design by repeating a single motif from a project, such as one of the basketweave designs on page 84.

1 Transferring the design from the chart square-by-square, draw several identical motifs on graph paper and cut them out separately, leaving a margin of one square all round each motif. Lay the motifs on a large sheet of graph paper and begin moving them around until you are happy with the arrangement. Try arranging the motifs in neat vertical and horizontal rows, exactly as though you were placing one motif on each square of a chessboard. This arrangement is the most simple type of repeat design and often looks very attractive, especially when the motifs are complex.

2 Next, move the vertical row of motifs at one side down slightly, so that the centre of each motif on this row lines up neatly between two motifs on the adjacent row. Repeat the movement on every alternate row. The pattern you have now created is called a half-drop repeat.

3 When you are happy with the pattern, stick the motifs in position using double-sided sticky tape or paper glue and make sure that the gaps between the motifs are identical.

4 When you are happy with the arrangement of the motifs, color in the different areas of the design with felt-tipped pens or colored pencils. Finally, make a color key at the side of your chart by filling in a small square with each color of pen or pencil you have used. When you have decided on a pleasing color scheme, write the code number of each shade of thread next to the appropriate square of the key.

Use this technique of drawing and cutting out each element of a design to create your own borders, pictures and samplers, and for working out the spacing between individual words or letters. You can select just one element of a large, ready-charted design and isolate it to make a small design. If you are designing a continuous border to stretch right round the edge of a piece of fabric, work out the corner design with the help of a small mirror angled at 45° (below).

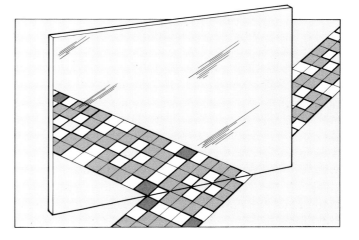

USING WASTE CANVAS

This technique enables you to work counted cross stitch neatly and accurately on fabric which does not provide a natural grid for the stitching, due to its uneven weave. Canvas is a stiffened evenweave material normally used for needlepoint, but here it is temporarily attached to the fabric to provide a grid for the embroidery. You can buy special waste canvas which has colored threads woven in at intervals to make counting simpler, or you can use ordinary needlepoint canvas, providing the threads are not interlocked. The kimono on page 113 is embroidered using waste canvas, and the technique will allow you to work any of the other designs in the book on fabric which is not evenly woven, including towelling and sweatshirt fabric.

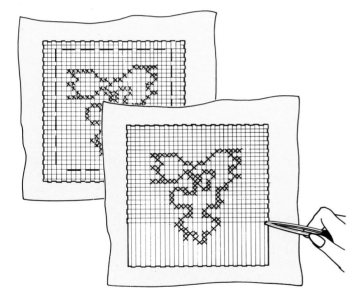

1 Choose canvas with the same count as the fabric suggested in the project instructions. Tack a piece of canvas on to the right side of the fabric, making sure it is large enough to allow the complete design to be worked. Work the cross stitch design over the canvas grid, taking the stitching through both canvas and fabric.

2 Remove the tacking and cut away the canvas close to the design. Pull out the canvas threads individually with tweezers, starting from one corner and pulling out all the threads which lie in one direction first. It may help to moisten the canvas with water first to soften the stiffening. Pull out the remaining threads.

WORKING CROSS STITCH DESIGNS ON CANVAS

Embroidery on canvas is called either needlepoint or canvaswork (never call it 'tapestry', since this is the term used for a type of weaving). Needlepoint produces a versatile embroidered fabric which, when worked in the appropriate threads, is extremely hard wearing and can be used to cover chair seats and stool tops as well as making lovely cushion covers, pictures and purses. Canvas is constructed to form a regular grid like evenweave fabric. Traditionally the canvas weave is completely covered by the embroidery, as on the Middle Eastern Star Cushion on page 133. However, on the Lattice Photograph Frame on page 110 some of the canvas background has been left unworked and other areas have been painted with acrylic paint. This more modern approach is not hard-wearing enough for furnishings but is ideal for purely decorative items.

A cross stitch chart can be worked square-by-square on to canvas without requiring adaptation, but remember that you will need to embroider the background as well as the design areas. Cross stitch (page 164) is a popular stitch for needlepoint, but you can use many other canvas stitches, depending on the effect you require. Square-shaped stitches are particularly good to use when working from a cross stitch chart and a selection of these is shown on page 167, together with two stitches which can be used to work backgrounds.

There is a wide range of threads available for needlepoint, and you should try to match the weight of your embroidery thread to that of the canvas so that the grid is adequately covered by the stitching. Further details of the threads used for the needlepoint projects in this book can be found on page 158.

Always work with your canvas stretched in a rectangular frame, either the adjustable type (page 161) or a wooden stretcher (page 161), since this will help prevent the canvas from pulling out of shape too much. An embroidery hoop is not suitable for use with canvas. When all the design has been embroidered, block the canvas (page 172) to remove any distortions from both the stitching and the canvas grid.

Before beginning a piece of needlepoint from your own chart, it is a good idea to stitch a small section of the design to make sure that you are happy with your chosen combination of fabric and threads. A small sample of stitching, about 2 in (5 cm) square, is usually sufficient to gauge the finished result.

EMBROIDERY STITCHES

EMBROIDERY STITCHES ON FABRIC

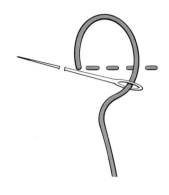

RUNNING STITCH

Use running stitch to work design lines and details when you need a lighter effect than back stitch (below) and also to decorate a hem. You can also use double rows of small running stitches to gather a piece of fabric. Both the stitches and the spaces between them should be of identical length to give the correct effect.

Work running stitch by passing the needle and thread through the fabric at regular intervals with an 'in-and-out' movement.

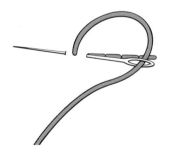

BACK STITCH

Back stitch makes a solid, slightly raised line. Use it for working design lines and to give a decorative edge finish to hems. This stitch makes the foundation row for whipped back stitch (above right).

Work back stitch from right to left, making small, even stitches forwards and backwards along the row, as shown. Keep the stitches of identical size.

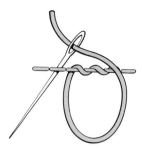

WHIPPED BACK STITCH

Whipped back stitch makes a heavier, more raised line than the previous stitch and it looks attractive worked in two colours round a hem.

First, work a foundation row of back stitch (below left). Using a second thread, whip over this line from right to left, as shown, using a tapestry needle to avoid picking up the fabric threads.

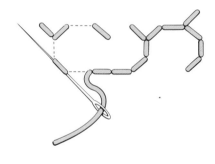

HOLBEIN STITCH

Holbein stitch is also called double running stitch. It is identical on both sides of the fabric and makes a flatter line than back stitch (left). On evenweave fabric Holbein stitch can be worked in a straight line or stepped to form a zigzag line.

First, work a row of evenly spaced running stitches (left) along the design lines. Then fill in the spaces left on this row by working running stitches in the opposite direction, as shown.

CROSS STITCH

There are several methods of working cross stitch on fabric, but remember that the top diagonal stitches should always slant in the same direction, usually from bottom left to top right.

The first two diagrams show cross stitch worked individually. This method produces slightly raised crosses and you should complete each cross before proceeding to the next one. Work individual stitches on fabric and all cross stitch on canvas in this way.

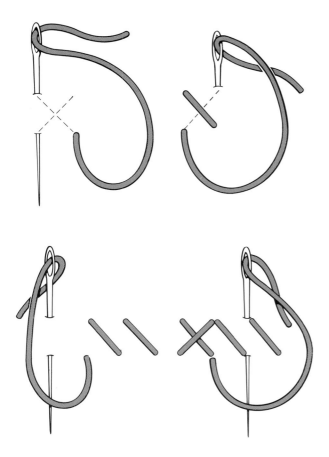

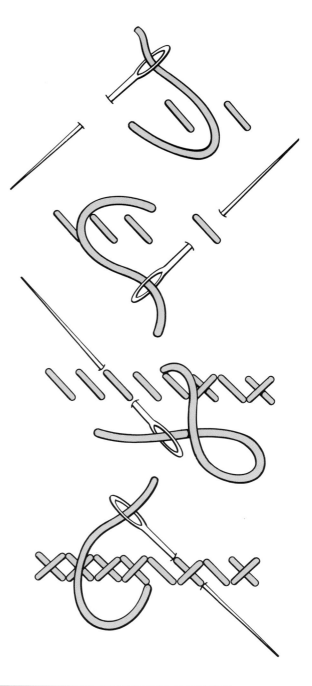

To cover larger areas, work each row of cross stitch over two journeys. First, work a row of diagonal stitches from right to left, then complete the crosses with a second row of diagonal stitches worked in the opposite direction. If you work a single row of diagonal stitches, it is then called half cross stitch.

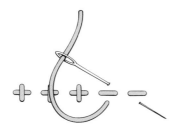

ST GEORGE CROSS STITCH

This stitch is also known as upright cross stitch. The stitches can be worked individually in the same way as ordinary cross stitch (page 164) or in a row over two journeys.

First, work a row of evenly spaced horizontal stitches from right to left of the fabric. Then return along the row, covering each horizontal stitch with a vertical stitch of an identical size.

ALTERNATE CROSS STITCH

This looks the same on the right side of the fabric as ordinary cross stitch (page 164) does when it is worked over two journeys. This method ensures a perfectly even stitch tension over a large area, although it uses considerably more thread than the previous methods, being worked over four journeys.

On the first journey, from right to left, work every alternate diagonal stitch along the row. Complete the diagonals on the second journey, working from left to right. Next, cross these stitches by working the top row of diagonals on two more journeys.

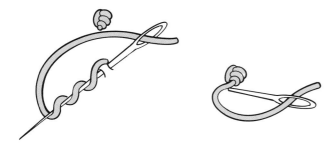

FRENCH KNOT

Use French knots to add texture to flat expanses of cross stitch and also to work raised details such as flower centres and tiny berries. Try working this stitch with three or four contrasting colors of thread in the needle at the same time.

Bring the thread through the fabric and hold it taut with the left hand. Twist the needle round the thread several times, then tighten the twists. Still holding the thread in the left hand, turn the needle round and insert it in the fabric close to the point where it originally emerged. Pull the thread through the twists to the back of the fabric.

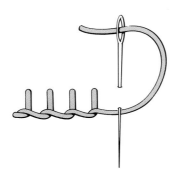

BLANKET STITCH

Blanket stitch is used as an edging stitch for appliqué and as an embroidery stitch in its own right. You can graduate the lengths of the spaced upright stitches to make a more decorative line, or group two or more stitches together. When the upright stitches are worked close together, this stitch is known as buttonhole stitch.

Work blanket stitch from left to right, pulling the needle through the fabric over the working thread to form the loop at the base of the row. Space the stitches evenly along the row.

EMBROIDERY STITCHES ON CANVAS

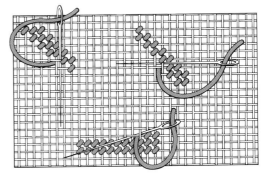

TENT STITCH

Tent stitch is also known as petit point and, worked correctly on single canvas, it produces a flat, solidly stitched surface.

Work tent stitch across large shapes and backgrounds by using the diagonal method shown in the diagram as the stitches are less likely to pull the canvas out of shape. Work up and down in diagonal rows, making small diagonal stitches over one intersection of the canvas threads.

Work lines and small shapes by the second method shown in the diagram. Begin at the base of the shape and work the stitches in horizontal rows.

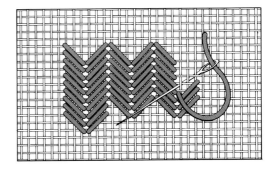

DIAGONAL SATIN STITCH

Diagonal satin stitch covers the canvas more quickly than tent stitch (above) and the direction of the stitches on adjacent rows can be varied to produce different effects.

Work diagonal satin stitch in vertical rows on either single or double canvas. Work each stitch over two or three canvas heads.

CROSS STITCH

Work cross stitch on canvas using the individual method shown on page 165.

CHEQUER STITCH

Chequer stitch is often worked over large areas in one color as it looks like brocade, but it can also be stitched in two colors.

Work the blocks over four vertical and four horizontal canvas threads. Alternate blocks of sixteen tent stitches with blocks of seven graduating diagonal stitches, as shown.

LEVIATHAN STITCH

Leviathan stitch makes a pattern of raised blocks which contrasts well with either tent stitch (page 166) or diagonal satin stitch (page 166).

Work leviathan stitch in horizontal rows from right to left, beginning at the lower edge. First, work an ordinary cross stitch (page 164) over four vertical and four horizontal canvas threads. Then work a St George cross stitch (page 165) of the same size directly over the top.

RICE STITCH

Rice stitch can be worked in two weights of thread.

Begin by covering the area with ordinary cross stitches (page 164) worked over four vertical and four horizontal canvas threads, then add small diagonal stitches across each corner.

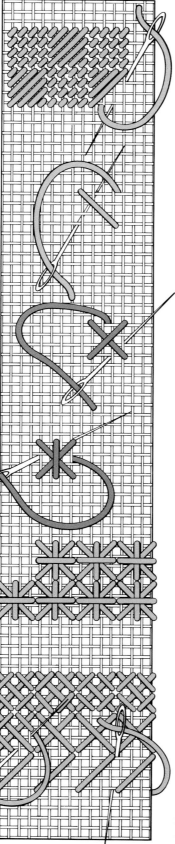

WOVEN CROSS STITCH

Woven cross stitch has a textured, almost woven appearance and it can be worked in two shades of thread to make a chequerboard pattern.

Work the stitches in horizontal rows, starting at the lower edge. First, work an ordinary cross stitch (page 164) over four vertical and four horizontal canvas threads. Overstitch the cross with four diagonal stitches which are woven over and under each other as they are worked. Follow the sequence of 'unders' and 'overs' shown in the diagram.

RHODES STITCH

Rhodes stitch makes a pattern of three-dimensional blocks and it can be worked over five, six or more canvas threads.

Work straight stitches across the block so that they follow each other in an anti-clockwise direction. Begin by working the first stitch from the bottom left-hand corner to the top right-hand corner. Continue in this way, filling every hole round the square. When working over an even number of threads, add a short vertical stitch spanning two threads at the centre of each block.

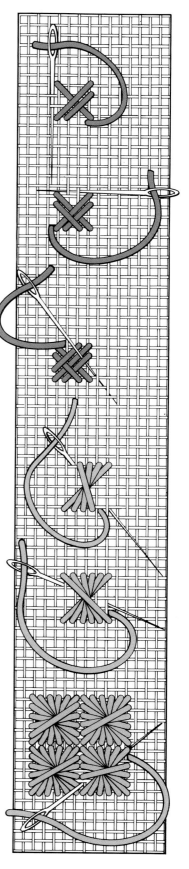

SEWING TECHNIQUES

SEWING STITCHES ON FABRIC

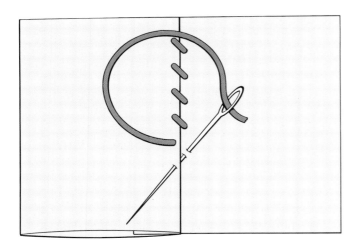

Secure the thread inside the fold of the hem with a few tiny stitches. Take small slanting stitches through both the fabric and the hem in one movement, as shown. Pick up one or two fabric threads with each stitch and space the stitches evenly along the hem.

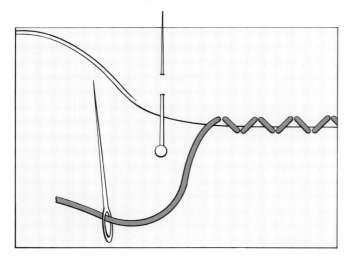

Use slipstitch to secure the edge of bias binding or to join two folds of fabric together. Secure the thread inside the fold and bring the needle out. Slip the needle along inside the fold, then pick up a few threads of the fabric. Gently pull the thread to close the stitches and repeat along the row. When using slipstitch to join two pieces of fabric together, work the stitch alternately from one fold to the other in the same way.

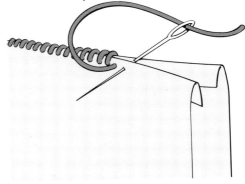

Use oversewing to join the right sides of two folds of fabric together where you need a strong join.

Secure the thread inside the back fold and bring the needle out. Take stitches through the top of both folds, inserting the needle at right angles to the folds.

This term refers to a row of hand or machine stitching worked close to the edge after a seam or hem has been completed, often in a contrasting weight or color of thread. The stitching is not only decorative, but also strengthens the edge.

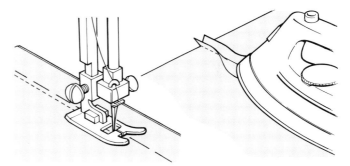

PLAIN SEAM

This is the most common type of seam. Neaten the seam inside garments by working machine zigzag along the raw edges, or by oversewing (above) or blanket stitching (page 166) along the edges by hand.

Place the two pieces of fabric together with right sides facing and raw edges level. Pin, tack and machine stitch ½ in (1.5 cm) from the raw edges. Remove the tacking stitches and press the seam open.

CLIPPING CORNERS AND CURVES

MAKING A HEM

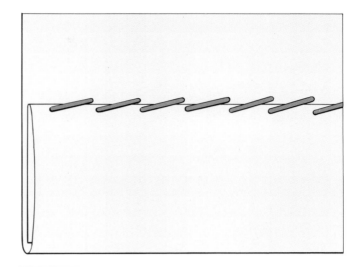

DOUBLE HEM

Make a narrow double hem when working with fine fabrics, around small items such as napkins, and also where you need a firm edge. Fold over half the total hem allowance and press in position, then fold over the same amount again and press. Make sure the corners are folded over neatly, then pin and tack in position and secure with hemming stitch (page 168) or a row of machine stitching.

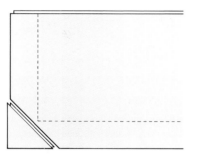

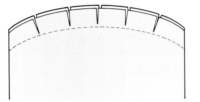

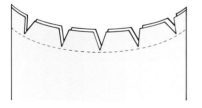

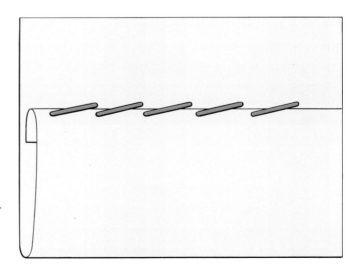

Reduce bulk by trimming away surplus fabric after stitching round a corner, as shown. After stitching curved edges together, clip into the seam allowance so that the seam will lie flat without puckering. On outward curves, make small cuts at right angles to the seamline, as shown, but on inward curves cut out small, evenly spaced wedge shapes.

UNEVEN WIDTH HEM

Use this hem on medium and heavyweight fabrics and for deep hems. Fold over the total amount allowed for the hem and press in position. Turn under ¼ in (6 mm) of the raw edge and press. Pin and tack hem in position and secure with hemming stitch (page 168) or machine stitching.

MAKING BIAS BINDING

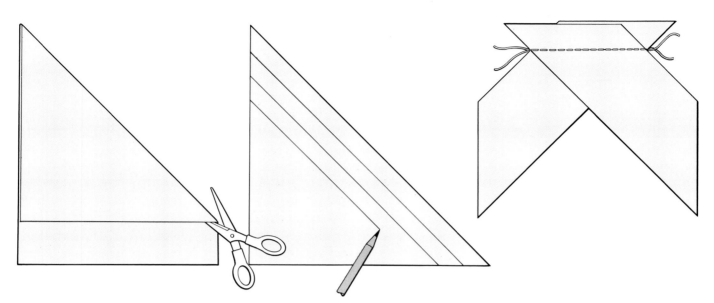

Ready-made bias binding is available in various widths and a wide range of colors, but you can cut your own from matching or contrasting fabric.

1 Find the bias of the fabric by laying it flat and folding over one corner at an angle of 45° to the selvedge. Cut along the fold.

2 Decide on the finished width of the binding, adding ¼ in (6 mm) to each edge for turnings, and mark parallel lines on the fabric to this width. Working from the cut edge, mark the lines on the fabric with a ruler and a dressmaker's pencil. Cut out the strips.

3 Join the strips together by placing two strips at right angles with right sides facing, as shown. Pin and stitch them together, taking a ¼ in (6 mm) seam allowance. Press the seam open and trim off the surplus triangular shapes. Fold ¼ in (6 mm) to the wrong side down each long edge and press. To finish, fold the binding in half lengthways and press.

APPLYING BIAS BINDING

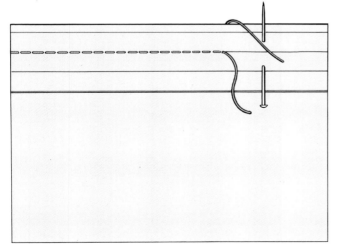

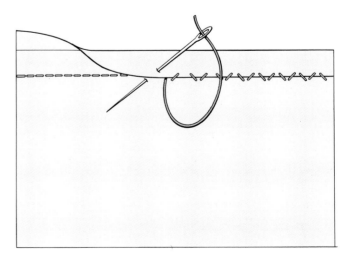

1 With the right side of the fabric facing, open out the binding and place the raw edge level with the raw edge of the fabric. Machine stitch along the fold line.

2 Fold binding over on to the wrong side of the fabric, enclosing the raw edge. Pin in place and slipstitch (page 168) along the stitched line.

MAKING A BUTTONHOLE LOOP

Buttonhole loops can be worked in different sizes: a small one will accommodate a button while a larger one can be used to secure a belt to a garment.

Make several stitches backwards and forwards to create a loop of the required size, then work blanket stitches (page 166) close together over the loop and finish off the thread end securely.

GATHERING

Gather a piece of fabric by working two rows of running stitch (page 164) close together. Knot one end of the thread and leave the ends loose at the other end of the stitching. Gently pull the loose ends and ease the fabric into gathers until the gathered fabric is the required width. Wind the loose ends round a pin to secure them. Pin and tack the gathered fabric in position, machine stitch along the seamline, then remove the gathering and tacking threads.

MITRED CORNER

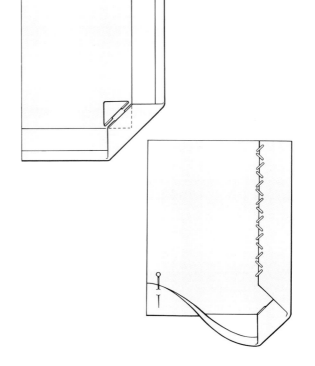

Mitre the corners of a wide, uneven hem to reduce bulk and give a neat finish.

1 Fold the hem and press in position. Unfold the hem once, then press the corner over as shown so that the diagonal fold falls exactly across the corner of the hem-line crease. Cut off the corner.

2 Carefully fold over one side along the hemline crease, press and pin in position. Fold over the other side in the same way. Stitch the hem, either by hand or machine, and finally slipstitch (page 168) the edges of the mitre together.

ATTACHING A WAISTBAND

Place the long edge of the waistband along the gathered edge of the fabric, right sides together, and pull up the gathers to fit. Pin, tack and machine stitch along the row of gathers. Remove the gathering threads and turn in the seam allowance along the remaining three sides of the waistband. Fold over the waistband along the foldline and slipstitch (page 168) round the edge.

FINISHING TECHNIQUES

PRESSING

Press cross stitch embroideries lightly on the wrong side with a warm iron over a well-padded surface. Cover the embroidery with a thin pressing cloth and press lightly so that you do not crush the stitching.

BLOCKING NEEDLEPOINT

When all the design has been embroidered, block the canvas to remove any distortions from both the stitching and the canvas grid. You will need a flat piece of soft, unpainted wood or blockboard ¾ in (2 cm) thick covered with clean polythene, rustproof tacks, a small hammer and a water spray or sponge. The wood should be at least 2 in (5 cm) larger all round than the canvas.

2 Hammer a tack into the centre of the unworked margin at the top of the canvas, stretch the canvas gently downwards and hammer in a tack at the centre of the lower edge, making sure that the vertical canvas threads are straight. Repeat along the two remaining sides, this time making sure that warp and weft threads are at right angles to each other.

1 Lay the needlepoint on the polythene with the right side facing upwards. Moisten the canvas with the spray or damp sponge, but do not saturate it. When there is a selvedge along one side of the canvas, cut several nicks in this edge so that the canvas will stretch evenly.

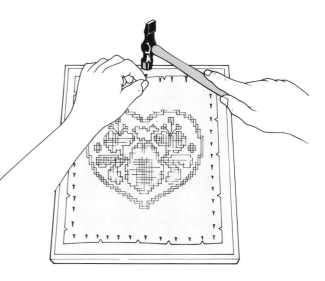

3 Working outwards from the centre, tack along each of the four sides, gently stretch the canvas and secure it with temporary tacks at 1 in (2.5 cm) intervals. Check with a ruler that the canvas is stretched evenly across both width and length, adjust the tacks where necessary, then hammer in all the tacks securely.
4 Moisten the canvas, then leave it out of direct sunlight to dry out thoroughly. This may take anything up to a week, depending on the yarn.

FRAMING PICTURES

LACING OVER CARD

Before framing, mount your picture over a piece of thick cardboard. Use a strong thread which will not snap easily, such as buttonhole thread, linen carpet thread or very fine string.

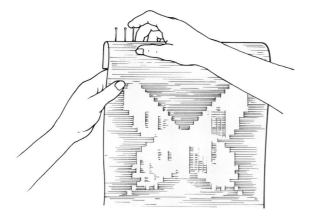

1 Cut the cardboard to the required size, allowing a little extra all round so that any embroidered areas at the edge of the picture will not be hidden by the rebate (overlapping lip) of the frame. Place the fabric right side up over the card, fold over the top and secure with pins pushed right into the edge of the cardboard. Repeat along the bottom, taking care to keep the fabric grain straight.

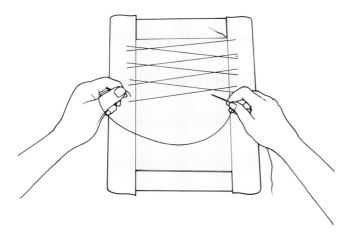

2 Using a long piece of thread, take long stitches between the two fabric edges, starting at the top left. When you have reached the bottom, remove the pins. Knot the thread securely at the starting point, then move downwards from stitch to stitch, tightening them as you go. Secure the thread end.

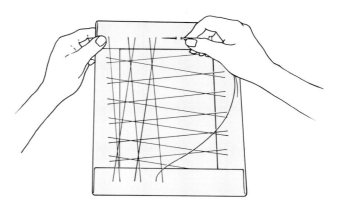

3 Repeat the pinning and lacing along the remaining two sides, folding the corners in neatly and tightening the stitches evenly.

FRAMING

There are several options available: a wooden stretcher, simple clip frame or conventional picture frame, with or without glass. Each of these methods has its disadvantages – for example, the stretcher method will not protect the embroidery from dust and dirt, while a glazed frame tends to obscure the texture of the stitching. Clip frames work well for designs without too much solid detail, but the glass presses on the stitches and flattens them. This type of frame can also allow dirt to penetrate under the glass and this will eventually spoil the fabric. When choosing a conventional picture frame, a window mount will keep the glass from flattening the stitches, or you can use small pieces of wood concealed at each corner of the rebate to lift the glass away from the fabric. After framing, make sure that the gap between frame and mount is sealed with gummed brown paper strip or masking tape to exclude dust and dirt.

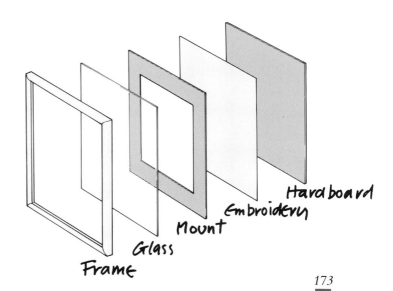

Frame
Glass
Mount
Embroidery
Hardboard

GLOSSARY

AIDA An evenweave fabric woven so that an identical number of vertical and horizontal woven blocks are produced over a given area.

AINRING Similar to Aida, but a finer fabric producing a larger number of woven blocks to every 1 in (2.5 cm).

APPLIED WORK See appliqué.

APPLIQUÉ A textile technique in which a shape cut from one fabric is placed on top of another and secured round the raw or turned-under edge with sewing or embroidery stitches.

BINCA A coarse evenweave fabric woven in blocks.

BLENDING FILAMENT A fine, iridescent thread available in a good color range which adds sparkle when used in the needle together with one or more strands of stranded cotton.

BLOCKING A finishing process for needlepoint where the embroidered canvas is moistened with water, pinned out to shape and left to dry.

CANVAS A woven material constructed from stiffened threads and used as the basis for needlepoint. The warp and weft threads make a regular grid. Canvas is available in several counts.

CANVASWORK See needlepoint.

CHART An embroidery design expressed as colored squares on graph paper and worked by counting threads to determine the placing of the stitches. Sometimes symbols are used instead of colored squares to denote different thread colors.

COTTON PERLÉ A tightly twisted embroidery thread with a lustre which cannot be divided into separate strands. It is available in three thicknesses.

COUNT The number of threads or woven blocks which can be stitched in 1 in (2.5 cm) of evenweave fabric. Also applied to canvas and known as the mesh or the gauge.

COUNTED THREAD EMBROIDERY A term applied to any embroidery technique on fabric which is worked by counting the warp and weft threads to determine the size and position of each stitch.

CREWEL NEEDLE A needle with a long eye and sharp point used for fine- and medium-weight embroidery.

DOUBLE CANVAS Canvas in which the regular grid is formed by pairs of vertical and horizontal threads. Also known as Penelope canvas.

EMBROIDERY FLOSS See stranded cotton.

EVENWEAVE FABRIC Fabric with warp and weft threads of identical thickness which provide the same number of vertical and horizontal threads or woven blocks over a given area.

FRAME An adjustable rectangular frame for stretching fabric and canvas while embroidery stitches are being worked. Two types are available – a slate frame and a rotating frame.

GAUGE See count.

GRAPH PAPER Paper with a printed grid of equidistant vertical and horizontal lines. Tracing paper with a printed grid is also available.

HARDANGER A fine evenweave fabric woven in blocks.

HOOP A two-part round frame for stretching fabric while embroidery stitches are being worked.

INTERLOCK CANVAS Canvas in which the threads are interlocked to form a very stable grid. Not suitable for the waste canvas technique.

MESH See count.

MONO CANVAS See single canvas.

NEEDLEPOINT A term denoting embroidery on canvas. Usually, all the canvas threads are completely covered by the embroidery stitches. Needlepoint is also known as canvaswork.

PEARL COTTON See cotton perlé.

PENELOPE CANVAS See double canvas.

SINGLE CANVAS Canvas in which the regular grid is formed by single vertical and horizontal threads. Also known as mono canvas.

STRANDED COTTON A loosely twisted embroidery thread with a slight sheen which consists of six separate strands. The thread can be divided and individual strands combined into various thicknesses.

STRETCHER A rectangular wooden frame which cannot be adjusted, used for embroidery and needlepoint.

TAPESTRY A term which describes a type of hand weaving. The name is often wrongly applied to needlepoint.

TAPESTRY NEEDLE A blunt-ended needle used for working needlepoint and counted thread embroidery.

TAPESTRY WOOL A thick, tightly twisted pure wool yarn mainly used for needlepoint.

WARP Threads running lengthways down a piece of woven fabric at right angles to the weft.

WASTE CANVAS Canvas tacked on to fabric to provide a grid for working cross stitch accurately. Special waste canvas is available, or you can substitute either single or double canvas, but not interlock canvas.

WEFT Threads running widthways across a piece of woven fabric at right angles to the warp.

INDEX

Page numbers printed in **bold** type refer to illustrations.